the Mother Letters

the Mother Letters

sharing the Laughter, Joy, Struggles, and Hope

Amber C. Haines AND Seth Haines

Revell

a division of Baker Publishing Group
Grand Rapids, Michigan

© 2016 by Amber C. Haines and Seth Haines

Published by Revell
a division of Baker Publishing Group
P.O. Box 6287, Grand Rapids, MI 49516-6287
www.revellbooks.com

Printed in China

Library of Congress Cataloging-in-Publication Data is on file at the Library of Congress, Washington, DC.

ISBN 978-0-8007-2408-5

Scripture quotations are from the Holy Bible, New International Version®. NIV®. Copyright © 1973, 1978, 1984, 2011 by Biblica, Inc.™ Used by permission of Zondervan. All rights reserved worldwide. www.zondervan.com

Published in association with literary agent Jenni L. Burke of D.C. Jacobson & Associates, an Author Management Company, www.dcjacobson.com.

Art and photography by Morgan Day Cecil.
Interior design by William Overbeeke.

16 17 18 19 20 21 22   7 6 5 4 3 2 1

To the mothers,
especially our own—
Susan and Tina

Contents

Preface   9

The Story behind The Mother Letters,
by Seth Haines

Introduction   13

Believe, by Amber Haines

The Mother Letters   17

A Final Letter   179

*The Truth in Weakness,
by Amber Haines*

Contributing Mothers   183

Preface

The Story behind The Mother Letters

I watched my wife, Amber, in those early years of motherhood—those days spent trying to sort out the beautiful complexity of child rearing. They were a whirlwind of feeding, cleaning, and conflict resolution. Exhausted, Amber would often fall into bed at the end of the day.

I also watched the creeping doubts sneak up. "Am I doing this right?" she asked. "Am I good enough?"

In the Christmas season of 2008, Amber and I decided we would create presents for each other instead of braving the holiday rush with toddlers in tow. A stay-at-home mother with three boys under the age of three, Amber needed a bit of motherly encouragement. So, I decided to curate a collection of letters written by mothers for other mothers. I hoped the letters would include words of encouragement and mothering wisdom while perhaps providing Amber a toehold for the hard days. And though I knew Amber—an unashamed lover of words—would appreciate this gift, I was not prepared for the response.

After collecting a few letters from close friends and relatives, I wrote to several of Amber's favorite bloggers and authors and asked whether they might consider submitting a letter. Within days, I received responses from Shannon Lowe and Ann Kroeker, each agreeing to contribute. Shannon, though, asked whether I had interest in collecting additional letters from mothers across the country. She asked whether she could promote the project on her blog, and I agreed.

The rest is history.

Over the next two months, letters poured in. Each letter represented a particular narrative, a different story. Some stories were joyful—the happiness of new life, the beauty in raising a child to maturity. Some stories were laden with grief—young children lost, older children estranged. But no matter the narrative, each letter conveyed encouragement, hope, and solidarity. Each story left one resounding impression—*we are all in this together.*

Amber and I have compiled this beautiful sampling of those first letters written in 2008, and we hope you'll find joy and encouragement in these pages. We hope you'll find strength in this collection, and that you'll pass that strength along to your sisters, friends, and your own mothers.

Thank you for being a part of the Mother Letters community. And remember, it needs your voice too.

Sincerely,

Seth

Introduction

Believe

Dear Mother,

When I first received the letters written by the hands and hearts of so many women, I said to myself, "I'm not even a mother. I'm a plain ol' mama." I had three small boys then, but I didn't know what I was. I felt small and like a copycat, a woman just barely getting by. I didn't learn to partake in motherhood until the voices who gathered at this fellowship table acknowledged me as one. What a powerful thing to be called: mother.

Now I've given birth to my fourth son, and every day I learn all the more from these letters, these voices of truth that have pushed me on to greatness. During my fourth labor, I found—with my swaying hips, with the way my neck held on to my bobbing head and my eyes stayed in their sockets—that it sometimes takes the full strength of motherkind to not push, to merely breathe. I found then that I didn't have to agree with the truth for the truth to be true. I am a mother, and a mother is amazing. Her love is a lion.

Though voices of doubt in my head said my son would never come, after intense hours of unbelief, after my dearest ones laid hands on me and their strong voices said, "Yes, you can," and after only minutes of pushing, there on the wild-eyed table was born into music and air my beautiful fourth-born son—

> and was also born a hush to my soul,
> the clarity of thumping hormones
> —the lick, the purr, the pink skin crying.
> The flash of ancient memory. Land of Milk and Honey.

Since then, with every passing, vigilant grog of night, through nursing and then when he didn't grow and we thought we would lose him, through weeks in the hospital, I had to come to the truth again and again. I'm a mother. I can do this—four boys, plodding ahead past the voices of doubt and toward voices of truth.

I push away that woman in my imagination who tells me who I'm supposed to be if I want to be "good," to be doing it right. I push away even what I think another mother's life seems to be, the vacuum lines in her carpet.

But here gather, mother, women who are for you, women confessing how little any of us know and how precious it is to be right where we are and who we are. When they tell me the truth about who they are and who I am, they change lives.

Your voices change lives.

I'm a mother, and I'm also a curator now. My husband and I have gathered for you in these letters the intricacies of a mother's life. We are art—and we make art. The rests we take, the line breaks. The images we snap with our phones and the ones we hold as the centerpieces for our minds. The scenes that reel and the way food lands on the plate—this is *art*.

In the image of our Creator, we mothers are artists, creating tiny people in our bodies and then gathering bits and pieces of anything on hand to keep them occupied. You should have seen my mama with a roll of tinfoil. You should see the artwork on my refrigerator.

Your story is a powerful reflection of glory. You don't have to believe it for it to be true, but by the time you finish reading this book, I hope you'll believe it a little more.

Believing for you,

Amber Haines

from AmberHaines.com

We all know they grow up fast. All the more reason to slow down.

~ ann

Blink

Dear Mother,

Blink

That's how fast it happens. I'm sure you've noticed it. When you brought home your newborn, you probably fell into some kind of rhythm and routine. Next thing you know . . .

Blink

Baby starts rolling over. And crawling.

Blink

Now he's toddling and talking.

Blink

First day of first grade: he climbs onto the school bus with a cartoon-emblazoned lunch box in hand, turns around to wave, smiles, and "catches" every kiss you blow.

Blink

Eighth grade: he shuffles onto the school bus jamming to an iPod and glances back, hoping you don't embarrass him publicly.

Blink

"Mom, can I have the car keys?"

Blink

You're shopping for extralong twin sheets for dorm room beds.

Okay, I'm only speculating about the car keys and sheets. I'm not quite there yet—but it's coming. Soon. I know, because I've blinked.

Blink

Other moms warned me about the mom-blink.

"Enjoy them while they're little," they'd advise. "Savor every moment now, because you just blink, and . . . oh, they grow up so fast!"

I appreciated the sentiment, but no one would tell me *how*.

How was I supposed to *savor* changing three-ton diapers, mopping spit-up off the kitchen floor, and chasing after my toddler only to find him splashing his hands in the toilet water?

How was I supposed to enjoy them while facing a mountain of laundry and so tired the only way I could keep my eyes open was to prop them up with toothpicks and guzzle a jug of black tea. *How?*

I'm the mother of two teens, an eleven-year-old, and a seven-year-old, so I can attest to what those moms were saying: they *do* grow up in the blink of an eye. But I would like to offer something no one managed to pass on to me—an idea of *how* to enjoy and savor the kids while they're little.

I suppose it sounds like a no-brainer, but here it is: *slow down*.

Does that sound obvious? Forgive me, but it took me a little while to "get it."

I had to *choose* to slow down enough to look each child in the eye.

I had to remember to slow down enough to smile, to laugh, to relax . . . to *breathe deeply*.

In the early days of parenting, I wasn't slowing down enough to listen to what my girls were really saying. I needed to learn to ask a follow-up question and listen a little longer.

I grew to love slowing down enough to read a story—slowly, more than once. And to play a round of UNO or Monopoly. (That takes awhile!) I love living slowly enough to sit down for a meal at the table and give thanks.

You might already slow down enough to let your kids enjoy some free time to play uninterrupted. You've seen them build an imaginary fortress or fairyland, and your schedule might be flexible enough to just hang out with them and watch them build. Instead of dragging them off to the umpteenth organized activity, you might be living slowly enough to take them sledding.

No, wait a minute. If you're already living that slowly, you know you can let your husband take them sledding.

While you sit and sip hot tea.

And while you're sitting there sipping tea, or coffee, or chai—not because you need the caffeine, but to enjoy the flavor and the smell and the feel of the warm mug against your hands—you are slowing down. You're stopping—stopping to savor these moments of motherhood that race past in a blink.

When you slow down like that, when for a few minutes you forget Mount Laundry and the blob of spit-up on the kitchen floor, life isn't such a blur.

Living a slower life, you can see things more clearly. You'll sit in the quiet and look out the window—really look—at the snow angels and lumpy snowmen formed by mittened hands in the backyard.

You can *feel*.

You can pray for your children—for their hearts, their souls, their just-a-blink-away futures.

And when you do this, when you slow down like this, it's okay to go ahead and blink. You can even shut your eyes for a few minutes and recall a look or a lisp or a laugh. You aren't missing anything at all.

Enjoy the peace.

Later you'll open your eyes when the kids and your husband tumble in the back door, chunks of snow dropping from their snowsuits and boots. They'll beg you for hot chocolate and popcorn. You'll look at their pink-cheek grins and chattering teeth and crazy hair smashed and smooshed by their knit caps, and you'll sigh. *This. This* is what those moms meant. And thank the Lord your life was slow enough to see it and savor it—and so was theirs.

This is how.

We all know they grow up fast.

All the more reason to *slow down*.

Ann Kroeker

Loved

Dearest Mamas,

When I was pregnant with my first child, my friend Emily (one year ahead of me in the baby-making) gave me a piece of advice: "Have grace with yourself," she said.

She was talking about those first moments when I held his tiny squirming flesh to my breast, when I expected fireworks of passionate mother-love and instead felt afraid, overwhelmed, and happy, exhausted and adrenaline-rushed. She said, "Don't expect the love you feel in that moment to be enough. You love your kid as you learn them."

Have grace with yourself.

I carried her words over into those first weeks and months of exhaustion. The long nights, the moments of fury at this little thing, whom I loved desperately but who was wreaking havoc on my brain and my body. I learned to have grace with myself when my friends were reading their four-month-olds books for thirty minutes a day and helping them progress in their development, and I still felt like it was all I could do to get my baby to sleep and eat and stare at me every day, much less be faithful to my calling and career.

Grace. Such a word for such an act. It's love, yes. But it's love that offers free kindness, freedom, acceptance. Jesus gives me that kind of reality. It's not an act that allows me free rein to ruin myself. It's an act that draws me in with loving-kindness, that sets me up to use my gifts and my heart and offer to the world what's good that's already been placed into my hands.

"Have grace with yourself," my friend said to me. She knew what I would feel some days: the temptation during my baby's first year to long for her success, to judge myself in light of her advancement, to value her in light of what the world values—appearance, physical impressiveness, signs of intellect. How often did I compare my kid with another? How often was I the one bragging of some sign of my child's superiority?

Have grace with yourself.

When it's your kid screaming on the airplane. When every person around you seems to think they know the answer. When you determine to trust your instinct despite his rage, despite your tears and the bite marks and the passengers who are tweeting about the horrible child and his incapable mother they are stuck with on the flight.

Have grace with yourself.

When everyone at the park is obsessed with getting their almost-two-year-olds into language-immersion classes, when your friend's three-year-old already knows how to read, when your strong-willed child is achingly sweet at home but yelling at the Sunday school teacher at church. When you're afraid no one but you understands him.

Have grace with yourself.

There might be a day when someone you love questions your parenting choices. There might be a day when you stare at your tear-soaked face in the mirror and ask, "When my kids grow up, how will they remember my failures?"

But motherhood is not a series of situations that have a wrong and right answer. It is a relationship. How many times have I described Jesus that way to one of the high school or college students I've ministered to? Jesus is not religion. He is relationship. Engaging with him requires our hearts and our minds and our souls and our strength, because it involves living, not simply rule-adhering.

Have grace with yourself, mama. This thing is complicated. You will hold that newborn and you won't know how to love

him, but you will and you will wonder, is this enough? And it might never be, but he needs you anyway.

See, that's the secret: you are his only mother. The only mother he will ever know. He loves you desperately. He needs you to love him back, to gather him when he crumples, to jump in the pool when he sinks, to snatch him up when the other kids are picking on him, to trust yourself to know when to protect and when to let him find his own way.

So gather her and love her. Laugh and cuddle and read and make choices. And trust that in spite of your imperfections, God is making all things new: even you, even your child.

There is refreshment in that grace: the chance to begin every day, the chance to learn and change, to stick by convictions and let some of them float away on yesterday's balloon. You don't have to be the same mother you were last year. You are being refined.

Once, another friend said, "Stop being so ferocious with yourself."

I'll say the same to you, friend. God has given you to your child and your child to you. And every gift you own combined with the strength of God's Spirit is enough to do this beautifully.

You might not be the mom who speaks two languages in the home. You might not perfectly balance work and mothering. You might not feel secure in the complexities of discipline and correction. You might receive every kind of judgment over the way you sleep-train your baby.

When it's all too much, promise me this: Walk your stressed little (okay, let's be honest, probably not-so-little) heinie to the bathroom and look in the mirror. Breathe deep. Look in the mirror again. Imagine Christ's hand on your head, and let his peace wiggle into those brain wrinkles. And say, "I am loved. I am loved. I am loved."

Because sometimes Christ's love is the only thing that gives us strength to love completely the little ones who have been given to our care.

You are loved,

Micha Boyett

Grace

Dear Mother,

I think back to my outlook on life before I had children, and I have to laugh. I remember looking at other people's children and silently judging, *My children will* never *act that way*. How prideful I have been! But now, suddenly responsible for the training of another's soul, I examine my own shortcomings, ask what faults I might pass down to my children if I don't grow and change, if I don't serve as a more positive example.

We as mothers are different, but we all share a common bond. We are a community of women. The fight is not against each other. It is greater than that. So instead of judging each other's practices, we should stand in support of one another. Let us teach our children love without judgment. Let us teach them grace and mercy.

And when we see a struggling mother, one who flounders in her role as "mother," let us not be afraid to offer a prayer, a hug, or a kind word. After all, we could all use the encouragement, and our children will be better for the example.

Love,

Christy Brockman

Calling

Dear Mother:

What do I wish someone had told me when I became a mother? It depends. Sometimes it has been something practical, like "Here's how to get a baby to sleep." (Here's a hint: swaddling and lots of nursing.) Other times, it has been something more intangible, like learning how to enjoy the small things or being present or giving up on the illusion of perfection. Those are all wise and good things.

But today, here is what I will tell you: don't forget that you are a person too.

This might sound like an obvious thing to say, but as a mama, I know sometimes it's easy to forget. After all, I have four tinies myself. I get it. We can bury ourselves in the care and raising of our children until we don't know who we are without them or we come to resent them for taking over everything.

Hear me now: I love my family more than my own life. And I cherish the daily rhythms of loving my tinies. I don't resent it by any means. But sometimes I know that it can feel like that's all we are—when all we do is serve and give and comfort and clean and cook and do laundry and soothe and nurse and entertain with age-appropriate flash cards, we feel like mothers *exclusively*. And that doesn't help anyone. Not you. Not your spouse. Not your children. And not the world God seeks to redeem in partnership with you.

Mama, you need to do the things that make you feel like a person. You need to stay faithful to your whole calling.

I learned this the hard way. Now I try to find the time and space in my life to do the things that are life-giving for my own soul. For me, it's my work as a writer, but it's also reading, knitting, being with friends, sitting on the edges of the ocean or the lake, being in the mountains, and browsing a bookstore. It is also wrestling with my faith and theology—even preaching, or pursuing justice and shalom for others in our neighborhood, and even around the world.

Being a whole person makes you a better mother. Don't become a caricature of a stereotype. Bring your whole self to this mothering thing—your tinies will love it and maybe even grow to love what you love. You will give them permission to love what they love and to pursue their callings too.

Share the things that make you feel like a person with your tinies. Instead of structuring your entire family around them—making small children and their interests the center of everything—make God the center and then equally value each one's personhood within the family. Include each other in your great passions and causes, likes and preferences.

If we want our children to care about justice and mercy and compassion, then we have to live it out. And if we want them to be fearless and bold and courageous, well, guess what? And if we want them to pray, we must pray, and if we want them to know God as love and Abba, and we want them to know that he is very fond of each of them, and we want them to forgive and offer grace and second chances and love tougher, well, then, here we go. We're about to live a better truth with our right-now lives. It's caught, not taught.

We're all different, and it's just a matter of finding what makes you feel like a person and—here's the key—honoring that enough to do it, both individually and by incorporating it into your family life.

It's so vital for you to find these pockets of your own personhood in the midst of the daily work of life together.

It is vital for your children to discover right now that they are not the center of the universe. Let them discover ways to entertain themselves—you're not their cruise director. Let them see their dad choring around on a Saturday and pull weeds by his side. Let them grab a rag and a bottle of vinegar to pitch in with Thursday cleaning. Let them read or go to bookstores with you. Let them come along with you to the food bank to sort canned goods. Let them send you off to work that you love to do. Let them see you caring for yourself just as you care for them. Let them come to know you over time as the whole, complex, amazing woman that you are.

It is good for the tinies to see you loving something and actually *doing it*. To see you being faithful to your calling, to see their other parent empowering you to do it with his enthusiastic blessing, lets them see you as part of your family's gift to the world. You'll enjoy each other much more, I promise.

Mothers are people too. Don't forget, now. Let your tinies learn what it looks like to be a person, made in the image of God, in the fullness of your personhood. Let them see that you can serve your family beautifully, fully, and still be a unique and fulfilled person.

May your family support each other in their work and in their callings and even in the things you all just plain love to do.

Cheers,

Sarah Bessey

Priestess

Dear Mother,

Yes, indeed, you are a saint whose name will be spoken with great love by great people. Being a mother is a precious gift. God ordains and blesses this work. Being a mother surpasses almost every other endeavor. My sweet mother-in-law once noted the importance of the position with the adage, "The hand that rocks the cradle rules the world." Your effect will pass to generations who will not know your name. The responsibilities and impacts are awesome, because the Source of the substance that is "mother" is awesome.

So here you are in this awesomeness. Often you sense that this world is too crazy, too out of control, spinning too fast—and you are exhausted beyond words. But this world is also filled with profound joy, ineffable exhilaration, and sheer amazement. At times, there will be sorrow, hurt, mis-understandings, things done thoughtlessly. I pray that you will experience it all, and that you allow your family to observe and share every possible moment. It is what helps bring significance to life.

You are not to worry; you are to trust in obedience. You are to love in ways that you do not yet know and might never understand. You are blessing and benediction, baptism and Eucharist to your family, friends, and neighbors. Thank you.

Love,

Becky Behling

Unexpected

Dear Mother,

When we found out our son would have challenges and would possibly leave us to be with God, I hurt in a way that I didn't know was possible. I would have done anything to make it better, but for the first time there was absolutely nothing I could do, nothing I could say, to change the situation. I would have taken him to a million specialists and sold my house a hundred times over if I thought I could do anything to help my child. It soon became apparent that loving him and being there was the best thing I could do.

How helpless I felt, and yet how much strength I drew from knowing God was in the middle of it. Knowing God said to trust even when I couldn't see the way helped so much. It was like holding someone's hand and letting him lead you while you walk with your eyes closed, trusting that he will watch your every step and guide you closely while you rest in his nearness.

The innocence of life was altered forever. Never again would I take a smile for granted, let a cuddle pass, or get too busy to see my little one for who he was.

Special care became part of our lives, and when those requirements became noticeable to those around us, I found myself not resentful, but rather feeling love and compassion toward everyone who passed by. I will never look at a mother of a child with additional care requirements the same. They do so much, give so much, love so deeply, endure so strongly, hurt so keenly, and appreciate life so much. At the beginning, I thought it would hurt to feel the inquisitive glances, but I was so proud of my little one that I simply felt compelled to smile—and might have even glowed when they looked. They might have felt sorry for me, but I could not feel sorry for myself. As a mother, loving a child with special requirements who draws so strongly on the gifts of a mother, is perhaps the most enriching experience I will ever know.

My little one has entered the gates of heaven, but I will forever be his mother, and he will forever be a part of me. As much as I would give anything to hold my little one close, my life will be forever richer because of him. It is only through

The handprints of our children will be captured on our hearts forever. ~Kari him that I have learned that the love of a mother is a love that knows no bounds, that knows joy like no other, that feels pain for another to a depth unexplainable. That would do anything for another without a thought of the sacrifice, that would be no other place than next to that little child, that can kiss a fuzzy head and draw so much from one kiss. That gains wings from seeing God grow in her child, that would do anything to fix a wound, and that would pray with joy, tears, and supplications more than for any other.

Through this, I have learned to trust that God, who made me a mother, equipped me to meet the needs of my special child.

Listen to what your children are teaching you. As you would sit and listen to God, sit and listen to the silence, to the things they do not say and to the things they do say. Actively listen to them. Make time to get to know your children—not just who you think they are, but who they think they are. Strip yourself of what you want them to be and look deeply into what God has made them, who they dream of being, who they are. Tell them often how much you love them. Kiss them endlessly. Hug them abundantly. Yield them to our heavenly Father; he will do so much more than we could imagine for them. Parent them intentionally and with purpose. Enjoy every opportunity where little hands seek yours and find contentment there. Revel in the snuggles after dark that provide the chance to hear the softly spoken thoughts from the bottoms of their souls. Breathe them in deeply.

I could continue, but I think the final thing I would say is to record those little moments you think your heart will remember forever. Every memory captured in time will be worth its weight in gold.

The handprints of our children will be captured on our hearts forever. They will shape our hearts into a work of art that only a child can create.

Love,

Kari Clark

Worry

Dear Mommy-to-Be, Veteran Mommy, and All of You in Between,

I have tried to discern what lessons learned or wisdom given over the past four years (since my launch into motherhood) has helped me the most as a mommy. Like many critical truths we learn in this life, they haven't been revelations that came in a loud voice from the heavens. They have been, instead, the quiet whispers of the Lord to my heart, soul, and spirit.

He has taught me that there is no fear in mothering that is greater than God himself. As my first son entered the world, we were in the midst of packing up our lives and moving to Bolivia. My life was riddled with fear. Fear for myself, but mainly for my son.

Would I be able to find what I needed for him without Walmart just down the road? How would I keep everything sanitary for him in a third world country? How would I keep him healthy and safe? How would I help him maintain relationships with his family back home? As we began our new lives, I increasingly feared the unknown and the uncontrollable factors of our new lives. I lived with this looming sense of anxiety for the first few years of our son's life. It robbed me of the reckless abandon I longed to have in loving my son and enjoying being a mommy.

When I was nursing our second son as a newborn, God spoke a beautiful truth to me. As I sat there holding my little boy, God whispered to my heart that these precious boys are first his, and then mine. *Who am I to worry about them when they're God's first?* Will God not take care of his own far better than I ever could? And can he not show this humble woman how best to mother his sons?

It really is amazing the fears that are dispelled, and the peace and comfort that it brings, in knowing I'm not alone in the mothering business. Not only do I have the wonderful earthly father of my children alongside me in the journey, but a heavenly Father who is with me in parenting my children every step of the way! Do the fears disappear? Do the worries cease? No. But they decrease when they are shouldered with both my husband and my Creator.

God has also taught me that he gave my sons to me for his godly purpose. I will be able to serve my sons unlike any other woman. It gives me a newfound confidence to know that I was purposed to be their mommy.

And in the same way, there is a godly reason that I was given these two particular boys to raise and love. They have made me a mommy, and in that, a different, new person. They have taught me the joys of the little things, the excitement in life itself, the gift of laughter so deep that it makes your tummy hurt, tickle wars so fierce you wonder when you'll catch your breath, playing chase from one end of the house to the other, and dancing together until you're so dizzy you can't stand up. *They have taught me that I am capable of things I never imagined.* They have shown me in new ways my strengths and weaknesses as a woman, mommy, wife, and daughter of the King. I will forever be grateful for all that they've taught me about myself and about this life. And as my father always told us, I will love them more than my next breath!

I pray for our journeys as mommies. I pray that they will be full and rich, that God will show us amazing things along the way. I pray that we will journey to a place closer to him, closer to our children, and closer to who he created us to be.

God bless,

Laura Bull

Courage

Dear Mama,

Here's my truth: sometimes being a mom stinks. I'm tired. I'm overwhelmed. I'm sick of the rigmarole. And when I begin to acknowledge that I actually feel these things, I feel like a terrible mother. Guilt rolls over me and sits on my feelings like an elephant napping on my chest.

I feel like a terrible mom because the other day I went to pick my son up early from school, and when I was asked his teacher's name, I couldn't think of it. It completely slipped my mind. And I looked at that secretary and I spewed out nervous laughter, hoping she'd be gracious at my complete brain fart—I've met this teacher at least four times—but all I could anticipate was her opening her mouth to start screaming, "*You are a bad mom.* Now beat it! You don't deserve to

What if being
a good mother
looks a lot like
being a brave
heart? ~Grace

pick up your son from school early if you can't remember his teacher's name. *Out with you*, and off with your head as well!" She gave me the name of the teacher, and I scurried out quickly, head hung in shame.

I feel like a terrible mom too often. Sometimes it's because I'm divorced. Other times it's my nine-and-a-half-year-old struggles to tie his shoes. I feel like a bad mother because many of the days I'm with them, I'm overwhelmed.

But then there are the good days strewn about; otherwise, there'd be no hope at all.

I hear you interrupting me already. "Well, Grace, let me tell you why I am a bad mom. I can beat your shoe-tying stories any day of the week!" And in fact, a friend of mine and I routinely get into these warped conversations of shame and guilt, each trying to explain who is actually doing the worst job as a mother. Are they productive conversations? I'm guessing not. Nevertheless, we launch into them like little kids running and screaming toward a roller coaster that will inevitably make them throw up.

The number of days I've allowed myself to sit with thoughts that maybe, just maybe, I'm a good mom? One. If you include today, as I sit here pondering all this: two. The number of times I have begged myself to consider all of this differently: to infinity and beyond! I don't believe I'm a good mom every day because I need to mentally wrestle myself to the ground to get there. Here's how it happens: I'll tell myself I'm doing okay. And then I'll attempt to do the things that would be considered "stuff a good mom does." I'll sit down with my boys and read the books at night, even though by the fourth or fifth book I'm nodding off. I'll hold in my anger when I'd like to say meaner things. I'll attempt to be fully present with the boys instead of digging deeper into Instagram or watching television.

What I'm holding to is that it doesn't matter if anyone else tells us we are good mothers; we need to say it to ourselves.

What if good mothering looks different than we imagined? What if you read the books during your nightly routine but seven out of every ten nights you inevitably fall asleep? What if you start the new, exciting, meaningful family traditions with pizzazz but sometimes tucker out? What if being a good mother just means trying to do the best you can amid feelings of tremendous failure? What if being a good mama means you try hard not to compare yourself to other mothers, even though you're still tempted to by Facebook and Pinterest? What if being a good mama rarely feels like success? What if it—*gasp*—never looks like Pinterest says it should? What if it very rarely feels right or even good?

What if being a good mother looks a lot like being a brave heart? If a brave heart means moving forward in the face of fear, can't good mothering mean moving forward in the face of self-doubt? And just like courage, I will pursue the actions of a good mother, even when I feel like anything but.

Hey, mama? I hope you will too.

Love,

Grace Sandra

Perfect

Dear Mother,

When you are bone-tired and soul-weary and you have little more to give, when you're defeated and whispers of "failure" tiptoe right past your ears and into your heart, listen and soak this in:

You are your children's perfect mother.

This has nothing to do with perfection or *being* perfect and everything to do with God gifting *you* to steward their lives. No other mother is better suited to be their mother than you. Their first home was your body, miraculously designed to sustain life, *theirs alone*, and subsequently there is no one—not even their father—who has a more intimate relationship with them.

For now.

See, there is a truth that wrecked me when my teenagers were littles; and despite hearing and *hating* it, it has informed my parenting ever since: You are not raising your children for yourself; you're raising them for someone else.

Understanding this while my children were still young helped me parent with an open hand. It allowed me to see the benefit of cultivating their increasing independence from me, allowing them a measure of self-sufficiency while under the care and keeping of our roof. It is a gentle nudging over twenty years or so that gradually prepares them to leave—and one day to cleave to someone else.

Your goal shouldn't be to raise adult children; you're simply raising *adults.*

I remember fearing the teenage years when our babies were still toddlers, bred by seemingly endless temptation and the cultural and peer pressures I knew they would face. Yet, maybe, this is the greatest hope I have to offer you: the teen years don't have to be dreaded or merely endured!

What is the best tip for parenting teenagers? Begin when they're born (though I promise it's never too late to start if this is a new thought for you).

It might be an oversimplification, but parenting with intention requires intention. My husband and I have given our children room to disagree with us as long as they are respectful.

We've listened when their opinions differed from ours and remained flexible if we were the ones who needed to change. We've affirmed our love for them and pride in them over and over and over, making sure they understand how we see them—as beautiful and perfect children for us.

And yet parenting is still hard, conflicts will arise, and sometimes we blow it. But even in those moments of "surface" failure, isn't the sovereign God at work in and through the circumstance to accomplish his will and conform us a little closer to his image? A kingdom perspective of conflict helps me to see its purpose, whether for me or my marriage or our children.

And after all of this—parenting with an open hand and with intention, delighting in the teen years—you will taste sweet and bitter when it is finally time for them to leave. Your heart will ache in new places, tears will rain when you least expect it, but it will be good and right and time. And you'll be able to let go because it's best for them for you to let go. Do you hear me? Let. Go.

It will come at personal sacrifice to offer this cheerfully to your children, but it will be one of the greatest gifts they'll ever receive. And whether or not they ever express it, they *will* be grateful.

So, my sister-friend, mama your babies with confidence, rest in the sweetness that for at least a little while their lives are yours to mold, and when it's time, let them fly. And grace upon grace, forever and always, you will remain their perfect mother.

Robin Dance

Learning

Dear Mother,

We try our best as mothers to teach our kids everything we can in the few short years they live under our roofs. But I think I've learned more from my children than I could ever begin to teach them. I've learned that if I really stop and listen, God seems to speak to me through my children. He reminds me of my childhood when everything was new and exciting and the worries of the world were so far from my mind. Seeing everything through a child's eyes just seems so pure and untainted. It is a breath of fresh air that keeps your sense of wonder and your sense of humor alive.

When Alex was about a year old, we headed off to the nearest daffodil patch to snap a few photographs in her Easter frock. I sat her down in the middle of the flowers in her cute little dress and hat. I thought Alex would look so cute holding one of these beautiful daffodils. Looking around, I quickly picked one and handed it to her. This came with a sense of urgency, of course, since we were plopped down in the middle of my neighbors' flower bed without permission, picking and swishing their flowers.

I handed her the flower, adjusted the hat, and was about to snap the shutter when she threw the flower down and grabbed a brown stick. Frustrated, and in a hurry, I threw the stick down and replaced it with the flower. She threw the flower down and grabbed the stick again. After several minutes I gave up and took the photo with the stick instead of the flower. Later, when I was going through the pictures, I realized that, to Alex, the brown stick was beautiful, and at least on that day more interesting than the flower.

That Easter Alex taught me something I had forgotten from my childhood. God created all things beautiful, unique, and valuable. As we get older we seem to let society shape what we consider beautiful and valuable, sometimes shunning the not so clean, not so pretty, not so great smelling, and the not so well-spoken. Sure, the flowers are beautiful, but I shouldn't be so focused on the flowers that I forget about the stick on the ground next to it. It would build a better nest, after all.

I've learned more from my children than I could ever begin to teach them.
~ mel

My son, Jax, has also taught me many things in his three years. Jax was born with a birth defect that affects his co-ordination, and he has been in therapy for the last two years. The doctors weren't sure if he would ever be able to walk unassisted. A few months ago, Jax shunned his rolling walker along with the braces on his feet and decided to play soccer. Three weeks ago, our family went to his first soccer practice. It is indoors and on a smooth surface, so we thought we would give it a try. He wanted to play so badly, and even though I was convinced he would be trampled, we signed him up. Did he keep up with the other kids? Not quite. Did he fall? All the time. Was he trampled? Constantly. Did he love every minute of it? Yes! I'd never seen him so excited. He had the biggest smile plastered on his face, and he just kept saying, "Watch, Mom!" He was the biggest klutz out there, but he didn't care nor did he notice. All I could do was cry and cheer. I never thought I would see the day our son could run, let alone walk unassisted!

Jax taught me that you shouldn't let anyone tell you what you are or are not capable of. If you love something, go for it! You don't have to be the best or even all that good; you just have to love it. I am reminded that anything is possible through Christ who strengthens me. God has been working a miracle in Jax, and he can work a miracle in anyone's life.

Listen to your children and pay special attention to some of those seemingly insignificant things that happen somewhere between breakfast and tucking them in at night. You never know when it could turn into a significant life lesson. They are hit-and-miss but worth looking for.

God bless,

Mel Thompson

P.S. This morning I spent several minutes trying to get peanut butter out of our remote control. I'm still looking for that life lesson.

Learn

Dear Mother,

Oh my, this is not what you expected. You dreamed of a perfectly healthy, "normal" child; we all do. You've known something isn't right, and now there is this "diagnosis," this label, this thing that states you didn't get what you expected.

Grieve, Mother. Go ahead and grieve the loss of the perfect child of your dreams. It is okay—the sadness, the fear, the worry, they are all normal. So pound your fists and have a good cry. The sooner you let it out, the sooner you can move on. Your child is the same, only the path you will travel has changed.

Love your child and educate yourself about the condition. Take little bites and compile a list of resources you can consult when you need additional information. Seek out families with children who are older than yours and the same age as yours. Ask them your questions and compare experiences, but remember, no two children are the same. Take what you learn and view it through the filters of your life and your child's personality.

Take care of yourself and be gentle with yourself as you adjust to the changes created by the diagnosis. Sometimes the best thing to do is nothing at all.

As your child grows, you will become an expert in acronyms such as IFSP, IEP, MD, OD, PT, OT, TVI and O&M, NCLB, ADA and on and on and on. Many people will have opinions, but remember that the one that counts the most is yours. You are an expert on your child. If a remedy doesn't feel right, don't do it.

One last piece of wisdom, and to me, this is perhaps the most important. Don't say, "You can't do that." Instead, allow your child the time, space, and tools to find his or her own limits.

The hardest thing in the world is to watch your child struggle, but it is these challenges that will build inner strength and develop the coping skills necessary to thrive as an adult.

And so, Mother, grieve the child you lost, love the child you have, learn as much as you can, but remember to be kind to yourself. Give your child the wings to fly, and someday when you are able, share your experiences with others.

Best wishes,

Lee Laughlin

(mother of children with albinism)

Patience

Dear Mother,

I was patient for her arrival. Knowing God was sending her in his best timing, for her and the world she was to serve.

We had waited, prayed, tried, asked questions, begged, and kept the faith for a child of our own for seven years. Each time I was at the end of my ability to be patient and trust, God would send an encouragement that I could hold on to, meat for my weary hunger. Confirmation that I wasn't crazy or dreaming up a plan that wasn't in his will for my life.

Waiting was terribly sweet.

It was chosen for me, the waiting. And I chose my response. I grew weary at the amount of "In God's timing . . ." I heard over the years of deep desire to be called "Mommy." I know it's true and best, but those words stirred up ugly responses, like a rake to my tender heart.

But God . . . he lavished grace, a bent-down hug when I stumbled into a pit. He gave me revelation that his perfect timing was not only for me but also for my future children—his little children. That someday their story would be in the Book with Isaac, Jacob, Joseph, Benjamin, Samson, Samuel, and John. All prayed for and believed for by their parents. All appointed for a miraculous time. All chosen before birth by our Creator, appointed to a specific position to serve in his Kingdom.

All of these, the ones that were prayed for, longed for, waited for—they all point to Messiah, the One we all waited for. He has come as promised and will come again. The waiting for his return is long-suffering, but Revelation imagery tells us it's worth the wait, even more than I can imagine.

So in this revelation, I waited.

And then the waiting was over. Seven years of waiting, and before our daughter took her first breath, God was receiving the glory for her little life.

No one has heard our story and not stated that it's a miracle. God's infinite time is not like ours. And when the miracle comes, the long-suffering seems like a blink.

I know this. His ways will include waiting. All miracles are worth the wait.

Even now I wait. I need another miracle to grow inside me, in the dark night of little sleep and baby rocking. My self cries, *Enough already!* and forgets about the beautiful miracle I have the privilege of caressing into dreamland. (Have you forgotten about the miracle God has given you? You know the one.)

She is entrusted to me, like each one of the miracles God has bestowed on my years. He asks me to steward her and all the everyday blessings he pours on us. He asks me to sacrifice my desires for his. He asks me to live like he does. He wants me to be holy like he is holy.

I cry out, *Lord, make me patient.* I know my impatience is an expression of my ungrateful heart. I scare myself sometimes in my impatience, how my temper can flare, how I grit my teeth, how love seems to vanish and patience is trembling with fear at my selfish rage. I want things my own way, in *my* timing. And pride is underneath it all. No matter if I'm tired or not.

We've all prayed for it. Asked for more of it. Wish we could start over after we've lacked it. Patience.

But love is first of all patient.

I wonder if it's possible to embody the other attributes of love without patience? To be kind, not self-seeking or boasting, to be humble and not easily angered—all of these require patience with myself, others, and most importantly, my God.

Sitting on my lap, she suckles nourishment from my body. I watch with amazement at God's design as she drinks in more of me. I am thankful and fearful at the same moment. I know myself. I know my thoughts. I'm nervous of how I'll react in the trenches of my new role as mama. I want to love her. I desire to be patient and teach her the same.

I'm amazed by my daughter's patience with me. She can't always communicate what she feels or needs. She doesn't set the schedule for the day. She is teaching me.

I cry out, again, *Lord, make me patient.* A still small voice rumbles in my insides. *You're praying the wrong prayer. Why do you ask me for an outcome, a blessing, rather than the One who gives? I Am. I am the One you need.*

While I waited for her arrival, he was the One. The One I clung to. The One who convinced me he was enough, no matter the outcome. I trusted him to be my only One. And now, while I wait to become less of me and more holy, he is the One. God is the One to show up when I'm too tired. He is the One to transform me into a mama. He is the One to grow my daughter into who he made her to be.

The Spirit reveals his fruits. He calms my heart and gives me peace. The first of his fruits—love—tastes so sweet. The second fruit he reminds me is patience, the very one I'm worried I won't have enough of to be a good mama to her.

God is love. Love is patient. Patience is fruit from him through me. God in me. The only way.

I cry out, *Lord, give me more of you.* Then, and only then, will I be patient. And with this, I draw near to him and he draws near to me. He is loving to me, and it looks like patience. He answered my prayer for my daughter and now is patient for her to know him.

I pray she will love him, serve him, and be fruitful. That she will experience his patient love by my hands. I will be patient, because of him in me.

Waiting patiently,

Stephanie Bryant

Trust

Dear Mother,

I don't know how to do it—be a mother, that is. Yet I find myself the mother to four little ones who, to my amazement, continually forgive me. It has been the avenue for my own undoing. I admit I don't like the way it feels sometimes.

But as time goes on and God continues to draw us into life circumstances where I certainly do not shine in my mothering role, I am realizing that I cannot do this on my own. It's a complete matter of trust, isn't it, that he will give our children what they need despite our shortcomings? Over time, I am noticing that I don't parent out of guilt or my own agenda as much as I used to, because I realize God has equipped me as he sees fit. Thank goodness!

I pray that your own journey into and through motherhood undoes you as it has me! It feels awful and wonderful and brings you directly into the center of the heart of God. It won't go smoothly, but I pray you experience the peace and sweet thrill of being cared for yourself by a heavenly parent who has no deficiencies or inadequacies.

Rachel McAdams

Needing

Dear Mother,

My journey of motherhood began much earlier than I had expected. I had completed my second year of college and was planning on going overseas the next year. I never got there.

That summer, I found myself twenty years old, unmarried, and pregnant. I was scared, mad, and unsure. But I knew at that moment that my life was never going to be the same. It wasn't about me anymore. God had different plans for me.

My daughter will be ten years old this April, and I, without a doubt, believe she was sent from heaven to save me. She is my pride and joy and the light of my life. She has blessed my husband, my family, and me more than we could have ever imagined. She has a heart of gold and truly believes it when she says, "God knew you needed me then, Mommy, more than anyone else, so he sent me to you early." And she's right. I did need her. I needed God to show me he was in control. She saved me. In every way possible.

May God bless you and your sweet, sweet family. May the memories you make each day be held close to your hearts.

Love,

Wendy Joachim

Seen

To the mother of the child with special needs,

I want you to know I see you.

One of the hardest parts about this job—raising a kid with an extra set of challenges, with special needs—is the seeming invisibility. We struggle the hardest at home, behind closed doors. Most people only see glimpses, if anything, but I see you. I see the weight on your shoulders and the love you carry for your baby. Our love is not unlike any other mother's love. It's just heavier.

I see you shuttling your kid to and from therapy sessions. I see you sitting behind the observation glass at the clinic, watching, wondering, *Is this even helping?* I see you sit through evaluation after evaluation. I see the extra doctors appointments. I see the tears when the diagnosis comes. I see you grieving the lost expectations, and I know the searing pain that you feel. I see you.

I see how you struggle to get your child to eat, because there's significant struggles with food and diet. I see that you can't go into a place like the grocery store without a lot of preparation and a lot of resilience. I see you sitting at the kitchen table at the end of the day, exhausted, tears spilling out and praying to God with a desperation only mothers like us can understand.

I see you scrolling through pictures of your friends' kids, knowing that your own child will always be different. I see the fight you put up, the one that battles hard against disappointment and instead battles on the side of joy and gratitude.

Joy and gratitude.

I see that you have a deeper understanding of both. I see the victories that mean so little to most people mean everything to you. I see because of the challenges you face, because of the challenges your child faces, you have a deeper understanding of joy, and I see the way you cling to gratitude like it's your lifeline. I see the way that holding onto the small joys will sustain you unlike anything else.

I see your faith. I see the way you question, I see the way you doubt. You're forced to ask bigger questions of God than most people would dare to ask, and I see how you're not afraid of those big questions. I see the way you push into them, with the goal of doubting your doubts before doubting your faith. I see how resurrection and new life and the promise of a new Kingdom means something different for you. I see it.

I want you to know I see you, Mama. I want you to know that it's okay to admit that this is hard. So often, too often, we want to sweep the difficulty under the rug and whitewash it with words like *fine*, because we're afraid of being a burden on someone else. I want you to know that it's okay to say it's not fine. It's okay to say that this is really, really difficult. You can say it to me.

I see you, Mama. You are not alone. I know, because I'm one of you. I imagine us sitting together, watching our kids. Celebrating the big things, grieving the hard things, holding tight to the joyful things. Our love is a fierce love, our joy is a deep joy.

I am grateful for you, Mama. You make me feel less alone, you make me feel more resilient. I know that somewhere in this big wide world, there's another woman like me who hurts like I do, who celebrates like I do, who loves like I do. I am praying for you. Will you pray for me too?

I am with you. I don't know you, but I love you so deeply. We're in this together, you and me.

I see you.

Love,

Nish Weiseth

Voice

Dear Mother,

I've always been a reader. My mother never needed to set limits for television or video games. Instead, she would tell me, "You've been reading long enough. Go outside and play." I was generally a compliant child, and our central battle was whether I could read at the dinner table. She wisely wouldn't allow me to drag whatever book I was devouring at the time to the table, and her refusal frustrated my appetite for words terribly. So I would obstinately read the back of the cereal box or the little flip calendar filled with Scripture from which we would have our time of daily family devotion and prayer.

Is it surprising then that when I became pregnant with my first child I read every book known to man—or in this case woman—about pregnancy? *What to Expect When You're*

Expecting, *The Mayo Clinic Guide to a Healthy Pregnancy*, *The Pregnancy Countdown*, *The Pregnancy Bible*, *The Mother of All Pregnancy Books*, *From First Kicks to First Steps*, *The Guide to Newborns*—the list goes on and on. All in all, I read approximately fifteen books in nine months.

"All the answers aren't in here, you know," my husband said after I handed him one of the books and asked him to read the highlighted sections.

"I know. But I want to be as prepared as I can. And there's really some amazing information in here. Did you know that if I lie on the wrong side it could impede blood flow to the baby? Or that some experts believe that if you rub my feet in a certain spot it can trigger labor?"

"Really? Great! I get out of rubbing your feet for forty weeks," he said, joking.

For me, a great deal of what I learned about my growing baby pointed back to Scripture. Psalm 139:13–14 reads, "For you created my inmost being; you knit me together in my mother's womb. I praise you because I am fearfully and wonderfully made; your works are wonderful, I know that full well." Jeremiah 1:5 reads, "Before I formed you in the womb I knew you, and before you were born I set you apart." With each passing chapter and new nugget of knowledge, my appreciation for the miracle that is life deepened. When I dwelled on the thought of my unborn son, when he hiccupped or rolled in my belly, I became more and more grateful for this beautiful gift God had given us.

Out of everything I learned, the most incredible piece of information was how important the mother's voice is to an unborn baby. Not only do unborn children recognize their mother's voice, they crave it—and will change their behavior to elicit their mother's voice. When I read this, I hoisted myself off the couch and went shuffling into the kitchen, where my husband was getting me a glass of ginger ale.

"I'm not crazy! The baby does like it when I sing."

I'm a classically trained soprano and had been doing a lot of practicing for an upcoming wedding where I was to be the hired soloist.

"I thought you said he punches you when you sing."

"He punches me when I *stop*. He's telling me he wants more!" I said, gleeful.

I've been a mother now for only five months—or fourteen months if you count the nine months of pregnancy (and I do!)—so my mothering resume isn't extensive. But one of my favorite mommy tasks is the nightly ritual I have with my son, Thomas. It's a cherished task because it shows how things have come full circle. It makes me feel both like a child and a mother.

When I was a girl, my mother would tuck me into bed and, in a low tone, hum sweet melodies to ease me into sleep. She hummed hymns, something she had learned in church choir, a Doobie Brothers ballad, something she made up. The melody itself didn't matter. What mattered was her voice. I wanted to curl up inside the vibrations; her warm tones covered me like a blanket. Her voice was pure love, and I was safe and secure. Once I was sleepy, she would quietly exit my room and go next door to my baby sister's room. I would roll toward the side of the bed, press an ear against the wall, and listen to her voice, muffled and far away, as she hummed the same tunes to my sleeping baby sister.

Thirty years later, with Thomas nested in my arms, eyelids droopy, body limp in surrender to sleep, I find so much joy in singing to him as my mother did me. I can tell that my voice nourishes him in a way a bottle never could. I know my voice gives him peace, gives him security, and that he hears only love in it. It's hard to believe that one day, probably when he's a teenager, this little baby will tune me out. Such is life and the natural order of mothers and sons,

I suppose. But I pray that my son will grow to always seek out God's voice the same way he seeks out mine now. Much as I made the choice to turn toward my mother's low hum filtering through the wall of my childhood bedroom, I hope Thomas will choose to be still and turn toward God's quiet but penetrating voice—the overtones of unconditional love and sacrifice from which all life finds its salvation.

Most love,

Leah England

Shepherd

Dear Mother,

I wish I could offer you some brilliant advice about how it all wraps up neatly at the end. But I'm still in the middle of it too—temper tantrums, book reports, permission slips, soccer practice, hormones, broken hearts, skinned knees—it's all still very much flying at me at a dizzying pace. It's almost too much to take in at times. The difficulty of being able to strike some balance and do the job I want to do—well, it mystifies me sometimes.

So the encouragement I can offer you is to tell you what I remind myself. Daily. Sometimes on my knees. Sometimes on my knees *and in tears.*

We're not alone in this journey. God has given us these little people to shepherd for a time, but they are his. When life is

We're not
alone
in this journey.
~Shannon

overwhelming and dark and exhausting, he is there. When it is precious and thrilling and magical, he is there. Isaiah 40:11 promises us, "He tends his flock like a shepherd: He gathers the lambs in his arms and carries them close to his heart; he gently leads those that have young." The first time I read those words, I wept. The God of the universe, the Master Creator, stopped in the middle of telling The Greatest Story Ever Told for just a brief moment to whisper, "Moms, I know it's hard. But I will lead you. And I will lead you gently."

So press on, knowing that he will shepherd you in shepherding them. Rest in that. Know that you'll fail sometimes, possibly even spectacularly so. *Trust him to redeem the difficult parts.*

And between the difficult parts? Laugh often, and hard, and unexpectedly. That goes a long way.

Press on,

Shannon Lowe

Fly

Dear Mother,

I have struggled with what to write because there is so much I would want to share: the pain of infertility and of missing someone you've never even met; the difficulty of a whimpering three-year-old; the awe of listening to your own little child's voice as she reads her first book.

But the truth is, the longer I am a mother, the less I know what you need to hear. So I have settled upon sharing with you the truth that guides me—that my daughter does not belong to me. That my job is simply to raise her safely and as happily as I can so she may fly toward a future of her making.

In the moments when my girl and I are knocking heads over whether she will wear a particular skirt or whether she will taste the greens on her plate, in those moments when my head really just wants to explode, I have to bring myself back to the letting go. Sometimes it is an hourly chore, for letting go is not my default, but rather a place I purposely seek.

I grew up in the warm bosom of a tribe that moves with the beat of accents and tildes, a people exiled from its own home and country. It was a childhood of many kisses, big sweaty gatherings with *tias* and *tios* and cousins twice removed, and so many delicious Sundays at the beach. I often wish I could give that same loud life to my child, save for some of the rules and expectations.

Even now, I don't know if it was because they're Cuban or just because they are who they are, but in my family there was a lot of "*porque, si*" and "*porque, no*," which basically translates to "because." Just because. I am pretty sure my tribe would not embrace the writings of Gibran.

While I do not wallow in regret—especially when it comes to the dance of mothering—I have a few "what-ifs" and times in my life when I bowed my head, followed the rules, and did what was expected, not what satisfied my spirit.

And so, as I look upon my dark-haired child—so curious, so headstrong, so much herself—I know my greatest gift to her is to stand by and watch her grow into whom she is supposed to be. She came through me, and I marvel at the knowledge that while in my womb she breathed because I breathed.

But she breathes deeply on her own now.

And the truth of that frees me to trust the arrow will land where it will.

Much love and peace,

Carrie Ferguson Weir

Presence

Dear Mother,

I am writing to encourage you, and I'm praying that my words encourage me. I'm just a mom, like you, with three young children. Except we spend a lot of time in the emergency room and making scenes at Walmart.

I don't know if I have any profound wisdom or life-changing advice. (Because frankly, while I'm typing this, my toddler is applying diaper rash cream to her hair. And my arm.)

But I will tell you what I know today:

I know God chose me to mother my kids.

I know he sustains me, grants me wisdom, and forgives the parenting mistakes I make.

I know the SpaghettiOs stain will never come out of my rug.

This is what it's all about. This messy house. This day. This moment.

~Kristen

I know *this* is what it's all about. This messy house. This day. This moment.

I know if I wait for it to get better, for my kids to get older, for my gourmet-chef gene to kick in, I will miss it all.

And I know I don't want to miss a second of it.

Kristen Welch

Brokenness

Dear Mother,

Isn't it strange? You sit down with so much to say, and then when you start to write, it's like whatever you were going to say just seems insignificant, or petty, or ridiculous. Will anyone even want to read it?

But here goes. I'll begin with the most crucial bit of information I have to share. I trust you will hear it with a receptive heart, because it is meant to give you the opportunity to have joy, peace, and hope throughout your life, with all its blessings and difficulties. I don't know what your life is like. I don't know your name, or where you live, or what hardships you face. I don't know if you are a single woman, dreaming of a husband and future children. I don't know if you are married, with or without children. I don't know if you've lost a child, or if your children are grown and distant. I don't know if you are a single mom, struggling to make ends meet. I don't know much, apparently. But there are a few things I do know: I am broken, and I cannot fix myself. Perhaps you can relate.

Just in case you don't know, or never heard, or haven't yet believed it, I want you to know we are all broken. I am. You are. We all are. Only God is perfect, and life without him is not life at all. All the wisdom in the world is worth nothing without that basic truth.

I lost my little baby girl this year: Janessa Hope. It feels good to say her name, to write it, and to know her story will reach you and maybe have an impact. You see, Janessa means "God is gracious." Her middle name, "Hope," denotes a trustful expectation in the fulfillment of God's promises.

We named her that the day we found out we were expecting a girl (at our twenty-week ultrasound). It was the same day we discovered she would not live very long. She had some severe birth defects that would quickly end her life. Of course, we were devastated, but because my husband and I had trusted our Savior, we understood that this loss could not rob us of our future hope, our current joy, or our faith in a God who does not change. We truly believe God *is* gracious, and we do have so much hope for our daughter and for ourselves because of what Christ has done for us.

We know we will see our infant daughter again in heaven someday. It does not erase the heartache we feel at losing her just twenty-one days after her birth, but it does ease it a bit. We watched her live with hope. We said good-bye with hope. And now we grieve with hope! I can't imagine going through this difficult journey without the knowledge that our gracious God provided a way for us to live in heaven with him and our girl, Janessa Hope, someday. The resulting hope carries us through these almost unbearably difficult days.

Did you know that one in four pregnancies ends in miscarriage, stillbirth, or neonatal death? Isn't that astounding, and sobering? I had no idea of those statistics before we started attending a pregnancy and infant loss support group after losing Janessa. That means that one in four of you mothers who read this letter might have already lost a child. It breaks my heart, and that is why I had to write what I did. I can't let you live without hope, say good-bye to that child without hope, and grieve without hope! It wouldn't be right, not when I know the hope God can bring.

I don't want to overwhelm you, and maybe I have said enough. Take my wonderful, gracious Savior's word and start living with hope. Finally, know that I am praying for you!

Lovingly,

Amy Lyttle

Blessed

Dear Mother,

I am a stay-at-home mom to an eight-month-old, with dreams to have more, adopt some, and maybe even one day become a foster parent. One thing I have learned in the short time I have been a parent is that my kids will always be better off when my marriage is flourishing.

We don't have money to go on dates really, so we make certain parts of the day our special times. We always make time before we go to sleep to pray together too. I have found that to be one of the single most marriage-improving things we have ever done. We also keep a notebook where we write letters to each other. We began it when we were engaged, and a few months ago we decided to start it up again. Love letters are a beautiful way to share your deepest feelings for one another, and reading over older entries reminds us of all the wonderful reasons we fell in love in the first place.

Motherhood is the most challenging, rewarding, amazing, life-changing, love-filled, incredible gift God gives us. Enjoy every single moment. The good, the bad, the beautiful, the ugly, the inspiring, the not-so-glamorous moments. Soak in every last one of them, because once they are gone, you never get them back. And thank God through it all.

My baby girl has rocked my world, changed my life, and transformed me from the inside out. Being a mom is the greatest blessing, and being a great wife and mother is what I truly strive for. I think if I can get that down, everything else will fall into place. I pray that your babies bring you every bit of joy possible, and that they know you love them more than life itself.

Meghan Matt

Motherhood is the most challenging, rewarding, Amazing, life-Changing, love-filled, incredible Gift.

~meghan

Seen

Dear Mother,

As I write this, I am pregnant with my first child—a little boy we've decided to name Samuel—and he's scheduled to arrive sometime in five to eight weeks (or so).

During my pregnancy I have been watching, observing you with your children—at church, at the grocery store, and at the park. I am watching, because I am in awe. I am always so impressed by the love, dedication, and selflessness I see. It makes me so excited to have my own little one, and it makes me pray that I can live up to your example.

I just want to encourage you by saying that when you are tempted to think what you do doesn't matter much, know that it does. In addition to the eternal impact you have on your kids, you have impacted me—even

96

though it is highly likely we've never met—just by your ability to love and nurture your children in that God-given way only mothers possess.

I watch you, and I trust that my God-given ability to love and nurture my baby boy (and our other children someday, Lord willing) will come about the time he does.

Keep up the good work. You will reap a harvest someday.

Love,

Anonymous

Live

Dear Mother,

My thirteen-year-old daughter looked at me across the table and said she felt like she was being rubbed raw by sandpaper. Life with her brother, who has FASD (fetal alcohol spectrum disorder), is not easy. She has lived with the chaos of his disabilities—lying, stealing, violence, and abusive speech alongside a charming, funny, and loving personality—all her life.

Friction scrapes away at the most tender points first.

I held her hand and listened. How to share with her what I am only learning myself? Thirty-seven years of living, and I am still a beginner.

How to explain that God's mercies are new every morning, that each day is unwrapped gently in the dawn, and each day's needs—yet unknown to us—are met before they arise, provision at the ready for those with eyes to see?

How to explain the penetrating power of gratitude? Its ability to rewrite pity into praise?

I fumbled through, sharing the reality of our options. We will walk this road to the end—no changing that. But we will choose how to walk: chained and bent by bitter disappointment or hands and face freely raised in praise. Our choice.

The answer to my own questions of how to share such truths seeps into my consciousness: words are nothing but air. It is the *living* that will tell.

Live it, mother. *Live it.*

Unwrap each day in the dawn and take God's provision. Eat and drink and breathe his presence.

Rewrite pity. Rewrite it into a rhapsody of praise and joy.

Walk the road, but look for the beauty along the way. And when you find it, rejoice.

This is how faith comes alive for my children. Not in my perfection or out of my abundance, but in my need. In the gritty realities of every day, faith shines like a jewel.

It is our living of it that will tell.

Tell it.

In Christ,

Tonia Peckover

Real

Dear Mother,

I am a mother, though most likely I will never hear a child call me Mom, Mommy, or Mama. When I was a child, I always dreamed of having children. I planned to go to college (check), start a career (check), marry a prince (check), and have a family (check).

It just doesn't look like I thought it would.

I am stepmom to three amazing stepchildren who have taught me more about grace and acceptance than I thought possible.

I am godmother and "back-up mom" to a beautiful, red-headed tomboy who carries my name in hers. What a truly precious and amazing privilege her parents have given me.

I am aunt to a niece and two nephews who delight my heart repeatedly, as we share joys and challenges, ranging from impending marriage to the exciting discoveries of kindergarten and preschool.

So, am I a mom? Yes. I no longer long for a baby to call me Mama, but I do carry a fading ache that my husband and I have not shared the joy of raising a child together from the very beginning.

Yet I know this is the plan for motherhood that God has ordained for me.

Like a "real" mom, I have loved, disciplined, encouraged, and provided.

Like a "real" mom, I have chauffeured, cooked, and attended soccer, baseball, basketball, and volleyball games.

Like a "real" mom, I have done much of it without recognition or appreciation.

Like a "real" mom, I have prayed and wept over these children by my husband's side.

Like a "real" mom, I have entrusted these precious lives into the Master's hands.

Motherhood isn't identical for every woman, but I believe that no matter what it looks like for you or what it looks like for me, being a mother is a blessing from above.

Blessings to you,

Elizabeth Walker

Victories

Dear Mother,

Hello! I hope this letter finds you in a moment of calm. It is a special privilege to write and share "mama life" with a kindred spirit I will likely never meet. I am completely unqualified to offer any advice, I am not a talented writer, and I lack the right amount of humor to tell a great story. Yet I looked forward to writing to you, and in the process I have focused on what it means to be Mom and how much we all need to encourage each other. So thanks!

What seems like such a long time ago, I was working on college admission essays with my dearest teacher. I was struggling to begin the essay that needed to address "My Personal Victory for Humanity." I remember throwing around big ideas about all the things I planned to do that would have an

Each day
brings its own
small
delights.

~Katie

amazing impact on the world. I dreamed of being a special education teacher and developing each of my students into proficient readers, independent thinkers, and world-changing philanthropists. I would be teacher of the year, travel to other countries to spread knowledge and charity, and, well, you get the picture! My dear mentor listened patiently and smiled in encouragement. When I finished talking, he asked, "What will you consider a small, everyday victory?"

I am still considering his question. I did enjoy a short stint as a classroom teacher before I decided to stay home with my kids. Now, as a mom of three little children, am I still working toward my own victory for humanity? I think so. In fact, I should take some time to appreciate today's little wins:

- I woke up from the first night our littlest babe slept more than four hours total (yeah!), feeling refreshed and ready to face the day.
- No one's breakfast ended up on the floor.
- My four-year-old earned a sticker at school for "using his indoor voice."
- I found the perfect pair of pink winter boots for my daughter at the secondhand store—just in time for the many inches of snow falling on our driveway.

- All three of my babes napped at the same time, giving me time to catch up.
- I had a chance to connect with you, another mom, which was a perfect reminder to me that there are other moms facing similar joys and struggles each day.

Important victories? Some. Exciting victories? Maybe. Rewarding victories? Eventually. I am reminded that each day brings its own small delights that eventually contribute to the great victory of seeing our children grow up to be joyful, productive, appreciative, competent people.

I hope the days to come bring you small victories of every type to celebrate and enjoy!

Thinking of you,

Katie Meyering

Cherish

Dear Mother,

This letter comes at a time when I could use a good reminder of what's important.

It's been one of *those mornings*. You know, one of those mornings when, no matter how badly you wanted to bite your lip and pretend your two-year-old wasn't running a marathon on your dining room table, it was indeed happening and required the "mommy voice" and stopping breakfast for the umpteenth time to get her down. One of those mornings when the sound of your four- and eight-year-olds fighting was like nails on a chalkboard, causing you to grit your teeth and take deep breaths, trying not to explode. One of those mornings when the baby wouldn't burp, and the oldest wouldn't come out of her hole (aka her room) to do her chores. And when, after sending five of my six children upstairs to get dressed and bring the laundry down, they didn't bring last night (as we ask them to do every night after their baths) so they could go outside and burn off some of that energy on their first of many days off for the Thanksgiving holiday, it began to rain. Pour even.

It was at that moment when I sat down in a chair, ready to throw in the towel and cry in my coffee, that my eight-week-old, about to get a boob in his mouth, decided to laugh for the first time. His first official time laughing, and oh, how he continued on! I stopped, met his eyes with mine, and continued to get him to laugh at me, at my breast, and it was awesome. It was just what I needed, my youngest and last's first laugh. That was the medicine I needed to make me right as rain again.

It's amazing how moments like that happen. I often ask myself why, when I've had a string of bad happenings in a row, particularly all in one day, when I feel I can do nothing right, all it takes to keep me going is that brief moment of sunshine, that sparkle, the emergence of that diamond. When my two-year-old says, "I love you, Mommy" for the first time, or, as I mentioned, my newborn's first laugh, or my eight-year-old scoring his first touchdown in flag football—it's moments like those that eradicate all the bad ones.

The bad ones are going to be there because our children weren't born with this innate sense for doing things right the first time, every time. Heck, when has that ever been the case for us? It takes patience to handle it all, and c'mon, some days we're fresh out and it's hard. I consider these days reality checks. *This job ain't easy.* Take a human and mold them into a decent, upstanding citizen. From scratch. This isn't baking a loaf of bread here. There are a gazillion moving parts you need to care for, encourage when they're down, teach right from wrong, wipe when they're drooling, medicate when they're sick. It's never-ending! But they are pieces of us, pieces of you and pieces of your husband, mishmashed together into this squirming, chubby, pink, squeaking ball of love that you smell and delve into and can't stop kissing, ever.

Then they grow—grow to smile, giggle, walk and talk, sputter out sentences and probably a few cuss words (accidentally, of course), learning to hit but learning to love and kiss and hold on tight. They grow to read and write and scribble beautiful masterpieces that adorn your fridge for the rest of your life. They will grow and get dirty and fall down and bleed and open up your heart and throw it around like a baseball a few times until you get their tears to stop and their pain to end by magically kissing it all better for them.

They will grow to suddenly think those same kisses embarrass them in front of their friends, but they'll still cuddle with you on the couch when a movie or show is on, and still climb into bed with you when their nightmare causes them 4:00 a.m. tears. They will grow and need you to take them to practices and be there for their performances, smiling and waving and taking a million pictures and probably embarrassing them, but it doesn't matter to them because you are present. They will grow and need you to buy them feminine products, and give them advice for their first date, and ask you not to walk them in to meet their friends at the movie theater, and need privacy on the phone with their friends.

They will grow and graduate high school and leave the house, and there will be an obvious hole in the house at the dinner table where they once sat, and you will feel as though you're missing a piece of yourself until they come home to borrow money, or laundry, in which case you celebrate their visit like it's Christmas. They will grow and ask for advice on their wedding gown choice, or ask you to go ring shopping to help them pick out the perfect one for their perfect one, and that day will come when you are the mother of the bride or groom, and you will inevitably cry those sad, happy tears, not wanting to realize that the small baby who oohed and cooed is about to start a family of his or her own.

They will grow to call to tell you "It's time," and you will rush to the hospital to be force-fed a proud cigar from your child proclaiming, "It's a . . ." and you will hold your grandchild in your arms and realize this child is the spitting image of your child, and these parents are about to experience the ups and downs and sideways turns with a little colic, spit-up, and a side of sheer happiness in the almost-same pink, squirming ball of newborn, just as you did.

Time goes by too quickly. Cherish it all, every single, solitary, stinky, burp-filled, grounded, first-date, boo-boo-kissed moment.

Love from,

Lisa Douglas

Miracle

Dear Mother,

It's hard to write a letter to someone I don't know. I don't know your name or what you look like. I don't know your hobbies or dreams or what keeps you from falling asleep at night. But I do know one of the most important things about you—you are a mother.

I am a mother too. My journey to become a mother was a long one, but my daughter is well worth the wait. She is all the best things about me, jammed into a tiny package.

My husband and I tried for years to conceive a child. Month after month passed and the pregnancy test was always negative. We underwent many tests, spent thousands of dollars, and tried to mend our broken hearts. And we grew closer to our God, knowing he did not make a mistake in giving us this burden.

With the help of several nurses and three doctors, I was finally pregnant! Oh, it was a glorious time. I didn't hate my pregnant body the way some women do. I truly marveled at this miracle. It's still amazing to me that I grew my daughter right in my own womb.

No matter how our children come to us, it's a miracle to be a mother. It's also a crushing responsibility; I have Perfect Mother Syndrome, although I believe I am recovering nicely now. I worked so hard at so many things in my life, trying to be the best. I had the perfect career, the perfect marriage, the perfect little house, the perfect circle of friends. This mother thing is a whole new ball game, though. Before my daughter was born, I had already read all the books. I knew *What to Expect the First Year* and how to have *The Happiest Baby on the Block*. It makes me cringe a little to remember how naive I was!

You can't raise a child by the book, though. My daughter cried for the first eight weeks of her life. I cried a lot too. What had I gotten myself into? I talked to the doctor and swaddled and shushed. Against our pediatrician's advice, I finally committed the worst mommy sin of all and put her into bed with us. I held her all day long. I followed my instincts. And do you know what happened? She stopped crying.

So this is what I've learned—and have had to relearn over and over again: I know better than anyone else how to take care of my child. No one knows her better than I do. I should always follow my instincts.

Oh, and I've also learned I am a good mother. Maybe not perfect, but certainly good enough. That's what we need to tell one another. You are a good mother.

Congratulations on the wonderful children you are raising. You are a good mother.

Love,

Sarah Hubmeier

Super

Dear Mother,

There will be days that feel like Christmas morning, when you wake up and look at your sweet children and feel so incredibly blessed and lucky, amazed that you get to be their mom, like opening a new package each time.

There will be nights when you check on them while they are sleeping and you'll want to wake them and kiss them and tell them you're sorry. For how the day went, for how you snapped or didn't have patience or pay enough attention.

There will be heartaches that will only draw you closer. There will be hard times that make the good times shine so bright.

And there will be love. Lots and lots of love.

There will be so many times you feel like you've failed. But in the eyes, hearts, and minds of your children you *are* Super Mom. You are their world. And you are doing a fabulous job.

Love,

Stephanie Precourt

In the eyes,
heart, and mind
of your child,
you are
Super Mom.
~Stephanie

Being

Dear Mother,

I am a mommy like you. I have four children ages four and under. As I write this, I am eagerly awaiting the arrival of Baby #5. People always say to me, "I don't know how you do it."

The truth is, neither do I. It's not magic. It's just . . . doing. My stepmom (mother to eight) used to say, "You just do what you have to do."

And she's right. Nobody else is going to change that poopy diaper. So you do it. And then you do the next thing. And the next thing after that. And you get through those days, one moment, one thing, at a time.

But it's more than just doing. There's *life* to be lived here. I remember hauling myself to my mentor's house and curling up on her front porch, begging for some wisdom to get me through. She looked at me and said, "Be still. You are in the valley (no, not of the shadow of death, although it feels that way between four and six every night). You are sitting beside still waters. Your children don't need you to enroll them in eight hundred activities, to keep the cleanest house, or to entertain them. They need you to *be there*. Practice the art of sitting. Watch your children play. You will never be a truly consistent disciplinarian unless you are on hand, right there, ready to correct and train. And that is what they need from you. To make them holy, not happy. To prove to them by your stillness that you will be there. That you are listening.

There are days to try to force yourself up whatever mountain of laundry or pile of dishes that needs to be conquered. But make that the only mountain you climb that day. *Simplify everything.* This is just a short span of life when your children need you right there. Not in the kitchen, not in the next room. *Right there.* Make beautiful memories of stillness and peace. Memories of Mommy being content to watch them play, to tie that Zorro cape just right, to laugh when they are silly. Make their earliest memories of their mother be of calm, quiet strength.

It sounds impossible because we have to strike this balance between *doing* and *being*. The things that have to be done will make themselves clear. And the rest of it? Well, that's where we pray for grace to make the right decisions. It took me some time to get used to not always being on the go, not forcing the days to fly quickly, not checking things off my list. It was far more an exercise in patience for *me* than it was for my children. But I realized that if I didn't stop and be still, I wasn't going to have any memories of their young days. It would all be one big blur of potty training and hunting for shoes and socks.

So we're a different sort of family. People think I don't get out much because I simply can't take my kids anywhere. This is not true. My husband and I can easily take them anywhere and avoid making—well, usually—more than one scene. Why don't we go out more? Because we choose to stay home and we train and we play and we *live*. And because Mommy tries to remember to "sit beside still waters."

Lora Lynn Fanning

Mommy

Dear Mother,

I am a mommy to a three-year-old boy. Yes, me! A mommy! That thirty-five-year-old single career woman turned wife, turned mommy. That eight-months-pregnant woman who, upon opening a onesie at her baby shower, asked, "What are these for, anyway?" I was a great aunt (unless dirty diapers were involved), who would have the nephews over for a couple of hours of fort building and sugar highs and send them home to their parents. But me, a mommy? With responsibilities like diaper changes and cleaning spit-up and doctor visits and enduring late nights and keeping another human being alive? Yes, me, a mommy, with a heart bursting with love for this little man who sees me get teary-eyed and hugs me and says, "Aw, you're okay, Mommy." A mommy who sometimes doesn't have time for a shower or a haircut or a dinner made from scratch but always tries to make time for that first sleepy morning smile, that important race happening on the train table, that guitar solo my little rock star wants to perform for me, and only me.

Yes, me—a mommy.

Love moments like these, mother. They are among the finest.

Love,

Monica Daughters

Transformation

Dear Mother about to Give Birth,

You have heard others say, "Your life is now over," or that everything is about to change. It isn't so much that your life will be over as it is that life as you know it will change. You might wonder how things that seemed so important no longer seem to matter as much. You might wonder what you used to do with all your time. You might realize your whole life now seems to revolve around another person, and that the very act of taking a shower seems like a great accomplishment. You might wonder if life will ever be "normal" again.

Yes, life will be normal again, but it will be a new normal—where love for your child will define all that you are and all that you do. You will transform from a woman to a mother. It won't happen overnight, but one day you will wake up and feel like a mother. Give yourself time to adjust to your new role; transformations do not happen overnight. Be kind to yourself. Get sleep whenever and however you can. Try to do something you enjoy each day—even if it is for just five minutes. Pray—if there was ever a time in your life when you needed divine assistance, this is it. Ask for help when you need it. Accept help when it is offered.

Most of all, enjoy your new baby. Right now it might seem impossible, but that tiny baby will grow up so quickly! Cherish every moment!

Patrice MacArthur

Fast

Dear Mother,

You love them—you really do—but oh how they can make you want to pull out your hair. They are so needy, so demanding and wickedly impatient. You are tied down and overwhelmed by their neediness, following a regular schedule that keeps everyone sane but can drive you batty at the same time.

I'm here to tell you that slowly it wanes, and one day you wake to discover that the child who once woke at 5:00 a.m. now wakes at 7:00 a.m. But he plays with his trucks until 7:45, which coincidentally is enough time for you to wake up and locate your happy face.

The child who would rarely get into her car seat voluntarily can now not only buckle herself in but assist her little brother while you load the groceries into the car.

The common refrain is, "Oh they grow so fast!" And all I can say is, "Thank heavens!"

Mine are both at an age where they function relatively independently, and this makes for greater familial harmony and more frequent family adventures. That's not to say we were hermits for the better part of six years, but our activities were necessarily limited. Now we can take a trip to the children's museum and fully enjoy the experience. No diapers, no naps, no bottles—just fun family time and exploration.

So enjoy the sleeping infant and the inquisitive toddler, but when the infant is inconsolable and the toddler recalcitrant, take heart that they grow fast and this too shall pass.

With love,

Anonymous

Growing

Dear Mother,

What a life we live. You don't understand it until you are in the role, and you wouldn't give it up for the world once you are there. You learn sacrifice, patience (maybe one day), and unconditional love—each of which is a work in progress.

Some days you think you cannot give any more of yourself. You are wrong. You find strength that you were not sure you had and make it through. Other days you can't smile any wider or laugh any harder. Your children will remember these days. The good goes along with the bad and makes a beautiful picture.

The good goes along with the bad and makes a beautiful picture. ~Sarah

Thank you, mother, for all of your hard work and faithfulness. The seeds you plant and nurture today will grow and blossom into something incredible, something worth all of your time and effort.

In Christ,

Sarah Huaman

Queen

Dear Mother,

Find some small fragment of time. Find a place where you can be alone with your thoughts. Close your eyes and remember who you are. Remember the time when you left home and went out on your own. You were probably a little scared, but excited and determined and joyful. Remember that feeling of "I can do anything" or "Watch out, world, here I come." Remember that you are capable, loving, giving, determined, and most important, a daughter of God, born to be a queen.

You have been given the great blessing of motherhood. Even with all the demands of being a good wife and mother, you are still of royal birth. Act like the queen you are, and your spirits will be lifted. Hug your husband, kiss your kids, and make family time a priority. Keep moving, and remember that there is joy in this journey.

Best wishes, remember your royal heritage, and God bless you!

Sincerely,

Tammy Zufelt Thomas

Within

Dear Mother,

There will be times when you look at your children in a mixture of pure wonder and fear. How do you let them spread their wings and thrive but keep them safe from all the dangers of this world?

Take a deep breath. Again. Reach deep inside yourself and know that only you can know what your children need. No expert, doctor, or well-meaning friend knows your children better than you do. Listen to that voice in your heart. And remember that the best thing you can do for your children is to take time for yourself to find your own balance. Your children will benefit from it more than you will ever know.

Blessed be, mother!

Love and peace,

a mother

Staying

Dear Friend,

Hang on to your marriage. While I was going through a tough spell with my husband, a woman who had been married for almost thirty years counseled me, "Just hang on."

At first, I had no idea what she was talking about, as I had not even hinted at or mentioned the fact that my marriage was heading downhill fast. When I asked her what she meant, she said, "I know things seem hard right now, and having small kids seems to make everything a whirlwind and stressful, but just hang on to your husband. Don't ever let go. It will all be worth it." I immediately started crying, because I already had started to let go. But I took her advice and vowed right then and there that I would not let my marriage fail. I hung on then, and I'm still hanging on.

In just a few short months, God transformed me and transformed my marriage. Our love has never been stronger. It would have been easy, even acceptable to some, for me to just walk away back then. But after walking through that fire, the depth of our relationship is something I never could have imagined just one short year ago.

So even when it might seem easiest to throw in the towel, just hang on. It is a thousand times brighter on the other side. And your children will be better for it.

God bless,

a mother

Matched

Dear Mother,

How is it that we can be so confident in our workplaces, in our friendships, in our ability to take care of a home, and yet when a child comes into our lives we suddenly start doubting ourselves? Perhaps it is because a child is far more important, worthwhile, and wildly consuming than any of these other things.

As a young twentysomething mother, I thought I had it all together. I was an educator, had recently finished my master's degree, owned a beautiful home, and had a wonderful husband, friends, and family. I was sure I had all my ducks in a row, confident in my abilities to be a mother. But now, although I wouldn't say I wake up every day with a lack of confidence, I would say I doubt myself far too often. I am learning that being a mother isn't about being perfect, but it is about trusting your instincts and making confident decisions. Being a mother is about recognizing that you were created to be the perfect mother for your child, and your child was created to be the perfect child for you. Being a mother to a precious child is recognizing we don't have it all together, but we were created as the perfect match for each other.

Mothers, we might not be perfect, but we are perfectly matched.

With love,

Heather Manifold

Enjoy

Dear Mother,

I once read that to be a mother is to forever have your heart walking outside of you. That is accurate and succinct. Motherhood is the greatest joy and heartache, all rolled up into one wonderful, messy package.

When our first son was born, I had an emergency C-section because he was in distress. It was my first (of many) experiences of frantic willingness to sacrifice my life for the good of my child. When our daughter came, I had the joyful and startling experience of meeting my clone, except much cuter and more artistic! When our second son was eight, he got lost in a new neighborhood looking for our dog and stayed lost for hours. As I told the 911 operator what he was last seen wearing, I knew unparalleled horror.

In turn, each child has brought incredible joy and many opportunities for prayer. In short, our children are not the extensions of ourselves that we feel they are so much, if not all, of the time (though we like to think they are). They are, in the final analysis, separate individuals and God's unique creations. They have great strengths and potentially disastrous weaknesses, just as we do.

Ask God to help you raise them with this view and with the goal of their being whole and independent of you while being totally dependent on him. Pray for them without ceasing. Hold them accountable for their actions. Be quick to apologize. Instill in them early a responsibility for caring for their neighbors; let them know that, yes, we are our brother's keeper. Teach them to prize family for the unique association it is, while realizing that sometimes a friend nearby is better than a brother far away.

When your children are grown, you'll look back and wish you could have done some things differently, but today ask God to help you do your very best and leave the results to him. Your time is the most valuable thing you can ever give your children, along with your prayers. Remember that the joy is in the journey.

Humbly,

Kathy Werntz

Anthem

Dear Mother,

You might not have grown up thinking you wanted to be a mom. You might have dodged clichés like "barefoot and pregnant" as wildly as any schoolboy dodges bruises and humiliation in the helter-skelter of dodge ball.

You might have prayed desperate whispers on your way to graduate school for a future and a hope where your degree would define you, not your uterus. And with a pocket weighed down by student loans, who could question your determination not to waste the opportunities of your education?

You want what you've learned to do to outlast how long it took to learn it. I know. I carry the same pocket change.

And now I also carry a baby on the other hip. My third.

I have all the bruises you can imagine that come with wrestling this life lived in the in-between. But I have not dodged the hard questions. I am not lost. Give me your hand, sister.

You will walk a thousand miles between this crib and this rocking chair before the sun comes up on a birthday cake with more than one candle on it. You will open the pages of a book—a friend that has made the long trek between your childhood and your womanhood with you—and discover that someone has practiced his lowercase letters in it. Unexpected graffiti will show up everywhere—your walls, your clothes, your car, your carpet, and most painfully, your heart.

But there are no mistakes. There are no accidents where life is concerned. Every beginning is sacred. Every beginning is good.

"In the beginning God created . . ."

Endlessly, hopefully, painstakingly he creates—waiting, willing, inviting us to join him.

We thinkers.

We students.

We writers.

We poets.

We wannabe degree holders.

We leaders.

We women.

The stretching doesn't end after the first nine months.

~Lisa-Jo

No book knowledge can prepare you for the act of creation or how brave you will become.

Nothing can put into words the discipline your excellent mind is capable of when your body is faced with the seemingly impossible math of delivering a human being.

No frame exists for the pieces of your brain you will lose through the toddler years.

God chose the foolish things of the world to shame the wise;
God chose the weak things of the world to shame the strong.
(1 Cor. 1:27)

Mortal words cannot capture the majesty of cocreating life with Christ. It is humble, yes, and messy and hard and will have you waking up one day wondering what happened.

But it is also an anthem. A thousand, thousand voices raised together across the centuries in the wild chorus of motherhood that soars over all you thought you would be and transforms you into all that Christ believes you can become.

The stretching doesn't end after the first nine months.

Nor does the joy.

And then you wake up one morning with barely room to roll over in a bed that's taken in strays overnight, and a small, tulip mouth exhales into your face. The day is still a whisper, and suddenly your body can't contain the hugeness of your spirit. Cupped in a tired mattress with someone snoring on the other side, you will live the cliché of the priceless moment and it won't feel cliché at all.

And when the baby cries and you get up and swing her to your hip and catch a glimpse of yourself in the mirror, it will all be there—the who you were as well as the who you're becoming.

And I promise, it will be very good.

Lisa-Jo Baker

Remember

Dear Young Mother,

Few things in life are as demanding and as rewarding as raising young children. Some days your sweet children love you to death. Other days your sweet children bug you to death. After hearing "Mama, Mama, Mama" a hundred times, you'll be ready to change your name to anything but Mama! Just remember that these precious children of yours are tugging on your shirt and pulling at your leg because they love you, they want you, they need you.

Your children cling to you because you're their stability in their unsteady world. They call you because they know you'll have an answer. They pull you to themselves because they know you can provide comfort.

These are the things mommies do: we love, we cherish, we comfort, we guide, we teach, we nurture, we feed, we clothe, we bathe, we answer questions, we kiss boo-boos, we hold, we hug, we forgive, we discipline, we train, we give. It's often thankless, repetitive, and less than glamorous. It's also rewarding, fulfilling, and a blessing.

Sometimes we have to remind ourselves of these things. Sometimes more than once a day. When you're up to your ears in mayhem or bodily fluids, it's hard to see how important your job is.

Remember that motherhood is more than dirty diapers and breaking up fights. As a mother, you're raising a tiny little person who is growing right before your eyes and will be ready to leave home before you know it. Every day, each moment is an opportunity to plant something in that tiny little person's heart that will stay forever.

Remember that this season of motherhood shall pass and open the doors to a new season with new challenges. We need not rush through this stage in our children's lives or merely try to survive it. We need to cherish the good moments, treasure them in our hearts, and enjoy this phase as much as possible.

Remember that God says our children are a blessing from the Lord, and that as a mother, you are blessed. When we serve and love our children, we also serve and love our God. The trials of motherhood are not only opportunities to train our children, but they are opportunities to grow in the Lord as well.

Remember that you are not alone. You have friends and family who see the work you are doing, who appreciate your efforts. Mothers everywhere are going through the same trials and successes you experience each day. Other mothers have already been where you are and are now facing new trials and missing these younger years. And Jesus is always with us, answering our calls in the middle of the temper tantrums, potty training, and dirty laundry we can't seem to catch up on.

Young mother, you will never be alone, your work is not in vain, and you are loved.

God bless you,

Amber Oliver

Kind

Dear Mother,

Wow. Even those words, "Dear Mother," are pregnant with meaning. I know that when I write those words, the mother reading them *knows* something of me. We share more than just a common experience. Only a mother can know about that yearning heartstring that bobs between you and your child. That feeling that a part of your soul exists in another, and that, quite simply, magic happened when this person came gracefully—and with wide-eyed trust—into your life.

And so I'm here to tell you something I've learned. Or, rather, something I'm still learning. I don't know whether my lesson will resonate with you, but if it does, I hope it makes you feel that you're not alone.

I have to be kinder to myself.

I have this habit of taking on too much. The result? Cranky Mummy. Rushed Mummy. Impatient Mummy. Exhausted Mummy. Unhappy Mummy. Who loses out? The whole family. Meals become snacks, washing becomes an insurmountable mountain, driving becomes a little too hurried, friendships are badly neglected, Mummy feels as though she's in a miserable pressure cooker, husband feels he's walking on eggshells and can't do anything right.

And the children—oh, those poor children—feel that Mummy doesn't want to spend time with them. They feel that they're "in the way," and they, understandably, act out. I really believe that our children are here to be our teachers, as are we to them, so I'm listening and learning.

Intellectually, I know I shouldn't take on too much. That I'm a sensitive person and need to give myself a good deal of rest between projects. That, yes, I like to give 100 percent to everything I do (relishing in the details), but that means I need to choose wisely the number and quality of things I take on. That, in the end, the only people I really need to please are myself, my children, and my husband. Yet I take on too much. Sadly, I know I'm not the only mother in the world to feel this way.

I keep being given this lesson to learn, and I'm more than ready to make this the last time it comes around. I truly believe there is a gift in every negative, and I'm getting much better at spotting that. In fact, it's almost automatic now for me to see the good in the bad, to see the upside of every situation. I really hope this is something that you, dear mother, are able to do in your own life. My own unhappiness with the "taking on too much" issue has been mirrored in my children, and I am so blessed that I'm able to not only see that, but to be able to create an action plan and new belief system that will help me change my behavior and automatic habits. It's going to make such a difference to the mood in our house, and I love that I will be showing my children how to live their best life.

So it's time for me to go to bed now—all part of that looking after myself way of life that I'm about to embrace. I know there'll be fits and starts, and that because I'm human, I might well falter and slide a few more projects onto my plate than would otherwise be healthy. But that's okay. I'll just course correct and make my way back to the calm, happy, love-filled space that is my home.

That, too, is my absolute, heartfelt wish for you.

Love and big, big hugs to you,

Joanne Newell

Know

Dear Mother,

Here are a few things I've learned in my first two years of motherhood. I wish I'd known them sooner.

No matter how challenging things feel to you right now, wait. It gets better. A million self-help books are eager to dole out the wisdom, correct the behavior, discipline the child, and so on. But the best solution? Have the patience and confidence to wait it out. Things will change naturally. Usually for the better.

Listen to your kids. Sometimes they're right.

Children belong outdoors. No matter how fussy the baby, how cranky the toddler, or how frustrating the preteen, nature puts life in perspective. Let a child teach you how to talk to shadows, study trees, and find wonder in the smallest details.

When all else fails, the sound of a vacuum will calm a tired, overstimulated baby.

You know all those well-meaning but frustrating people who tell you, "They grow up so fast, so enjoy it now" when you're sleep deprived, exhausted, and cranky? They were right.

Follow your instincts.

Birth stories are empowering, transforming, and irreplaceable. For better or worse, embrace yours. Or let it go.

Get down on the floor and play with your kids now. Laundry, dishes, and chores really can wait.

Your time is always the best gift. A plain cardboard box runs a close second.

Cook and garden with your child. A love of wholesome, real food begins here.

Talk to strangers.

Cultivate compassion. The rest follows.

Love,

Anonymous

Surprises

Dear Mom,

Buckle up and get ready—you are in for the ride of your life. Motherhood is everything I ever dreamed it would be and a million things I never expected.

I knew I would love any children I had. I didn't know I would feel as though my heart would forever exist outside my body, carried around by small people who sling it over their shoulders like a backpack.

I knew I would worry. I didn't know the worry would some-times be a physical pain—like lying on your back as someone sits directly on your chest. I didn't know I would worry about *all* children the way I do.

I knew I would lose sleep. I didn't know I would think those midnight-sleepless-moments would be some of the dearest to me—snuggling a sleeping child is as close to heaven as I have been.

I knew my kids would make me laugh. I didn't know I would giggle like a five-year-old being tickled to death. I didn't know the laughter would remind me what it feels like to lose your breath to a fit of chuckles.

I knew I would play with my kids. I didn't know I would enjoy it so much. I definitely never pictured myself running and ducking around the outside of the car while parked at the gas station—all in the hopes of eliciting those high-pitched kiddo giggles.

I knew I would have proud moments. I didn't know those moments would happen almost daily (for smiling, holding a crayon, writing the letter *M*, recognizing a flower, hitting a baseball), and I didn't know it would feel like the pride was bubbling up under my skin, threatening to explode on the nearest person.

I figured I would bond with other mothers. I didn't realize that bond would be like superglue. Becoming a mother is a one-way ticket into a truly magnificent sisterhood. These other mothers guide, encourage, commiserate, and share with me every step of the way.

I always knew I loved my alone time. I didn't understand the scope of alone time until I had gone a full week without

Motherhood is everything I ever dreamed it would be and a million things I never expected.

~Danielle

showering or using the bathroom by myself. I now know I occasionally need some time alone—it makes me a better mother.

I was positive I would stick to my list of all the things I would never say and do "when I am a parent." My kids are still little, and I am slowly working my way through each and every one. "Because I said so" and "Because I am the mommy" are, in fact, reasonable things to say.

I've been told to appreciate each moment, but until I had my small ones, I never understood how fragile those moments could be.

I knew life would be different. I didn't know I would never, ever again be the same. And I am a better person for it. Being a mommy is a job. It is the best one you will ever have, and it is the most important one you will ever have. You will learn from your children as much as you will teach them.

The key to being extraordinary in this job, I believe, is to keep trying.

Much love,

Danielle Elliot Smith

Meltdown

Dear Mother,

A few weeks ago I started to compose a letter to my children, and then something happened. I kind of lost it in a "Mama's having a meltdown" kind of way. I wanted to write this beautiful letter of how motherhood has changed me for the better and how these children are the lights of my life. I wanted to write how everything is perfect and grand. Frankly, I wanted to lie.

After my meltdown, I got in my van and drove for a while (three whole hours), and when I got home I trudged up the stairs, embarrassed by my behavior. I got in a hot shower and sobbed. The tears met with the streaming water but, oddly, neither had a cleansing effect. It was in *that* moment that I decided to hit the road for one of our big road trips back to our hometown of Buffalo, New York. Certainly I would see the true meaning of what it meant to be a mother by getting into a van with my children. My hope was that in nine hundred miles I would figure things out.

I packed us up, and early one Sunday morning we set off. When I cranked up the van, we heard a man on the radio say, "Have you tried peace?" And it became our trip's motto (it would become much more in actuality). Fifteen hours together in a van makes us all a little crazy, so what better than trying peace? If someone got a little cuckoo, another would pipe up asking if the crazy one tried peace. At one point I was feeling a little frustrated at the noise level. The frustration was overly apparent.

"Hey, Mama, have you tried peace?" my third-born son, Benjamin, asked.

"No, Benny. I forgot to try it," I answered, bluntly.

"Well, try it. You know, peace is really good," he reminded me. He was right.

Thinking about what I'd write today, I realized that I wasn't doing anyone justice by sugarcoating and stating that this life we live together is all rainbows and ribbons and pink lemonade. It's not; it's chock-full of obstacles, worry, doubt, and frustration. Even with all of that, however, we have a wonderful, hardcore love among us. We have music flowing freely. We have laughter that infects us to the point of stomachs aching. We have hugs that are tight, and we have kisses that are nonstop.

Nothing is perfect, nor should it be. If it was perfect, it would be a lie. And that's why I scrapped that first letter. I could easily talk about the beauty of it all. I realize, though, that the grit of life *is* the beauty. Without it we would be nothing. So now I just strive for peace. Peace in the knowledge that as we go through this hectic, crazy, strange life, we are bound by a love that is indescribable. Peace in the fact that these four entities I pushed through my loins into the world were made out of love. Peace in knowing that, while insanity might strike us daily, with all our flaws, with all our troubles, with all our being, *we are what we are.*

Have you tried peace?

I'm trying. I really am. Daily. It's the best I can do. It's the best we all can do.

Love,

Mishelle Lane

Empathy

Dear First-Time Mother,

There are millions of wonderful things about being a first-time mom. There are also a handful of things that no one really prepares you for.

You have no idea what the term *sleep deprivation* really means until you fall asleep talking to your best friend on the phone. You have no idea how guilty you'll feel when your baby is crying hysterically and you can't fix it right away. You have no idea that such a tiny baby can make his or her last meal hit the wall across the room after a little too much bouncing around. No idea!

It's on-the-job training at its finest!

In addition to all that sort of stuff, I was quite unprepared for all the unsolicited advice and opinions that were about to come my way. As if first-time parenthood weren't stressful enough, try adding in all the well-meaning (and sometimes rather snarky) opinions of both your closest friends and total strangers. Don't get me wrong. I got some great pieces of advice along the way (still do), and I love passing along ideas that have helped me as I navigate this road. I feel like I have finally (on my third go-round) become confident enough to filter it all appropriately. Mothering, in my opinion, is an art, and it takes a while to get it. One of those live-and-learn deals.

But after all this time, one thing still sort of ruffles my feathers. Something I like to call *random acts of judgment*.

I have gained great perspective following the few occasions I have had to deal with this phenomenon, and I think these experiences have taught me more (more than anything else) about what I want to be as a mother—or should I say, what I *don't* want to be. Each time it happens, I remind myself to be more tolerant, to think before I speak, and to remember that I don't know it all. It reminds me to pray for patience and for the person who commits the act.

Let me just give you an example of one such random act of judgment.

One gorgeous spring day about two years ago, my daughter, Lucy, and I had a big day planned. On Thursday mornings, Lucy took a ballet class at a fun little studio in a neighboring town. We would have a great time on those days, and I would usually treat her to a yummy lunch after class. It was rare to have this alone time with my second born, and I always tried to make a big deal out of our time together.

This particular day we decided to try the brand-new Whole Foods café. They have an awesome lunch selection, and I had already told Lucy she could pick out whatever she wanted. We sang songs the whole way to the store and we laughed about something silly Daddy had done. She said, "How 'bout if we call Daddy to see if he can come too?" What a treat it would be to have Mommy *and* Daddy all to herself!

I couldn't get Chris on the phone, so I left a message and told Lucy that he might call us back to say he could join us. We made it to Whole Foods and walked all over the store picking out every yummy thing we could imagine. It was so much fun.

The store was busy that day, and we were hoping to get a seat outside. But by the time we were ready to sit down, the only seats left were right by the checkout counter. We settled into a little booth, and I opened Lucy's milk and cut up her pizza and cantaloupe. She was famished by this point and couldn't wait to dig in. I even promised her a treat from the bakery if she ate well (if you know Lucy at all, you know she has a love affair with sweets).

Just as she was getting started, Chris called. Literally *seconds* after I picked up the phone, a little old lady passed by our table. I had all but said, "Hey, what's up?" when she lit *me* up!

"*You* should be ashamed of yourself! You need to get off that phone and pay attention to that *precious little girl*!"

And like that, she was gone. Poof. Done.

Every head turned in my direction. People were whispering and shaking their heads, looking at me as if I had just beaten my child or something. I was in shock, embarrassed, and basically blown away.

Had that lady been there when I played Lucy's favorite song over and over in the car? Was she there when I called her daddy to ask him to join us? What if that phone call was from my son's teacher, telling me he was sick? What if Chris had been in a car accident?

A million scenarios raced through my head. The more I thought about it, the more angry I became. I was appalled, shocked, and amazed at the flippant judgment others can place upon us in situations they know nothing about. I thought about it off and on for weeks. I told all my closest friends how horrible it made me feel, how I felt so misunderstood and unjustly judged. I was angry and irritated. When your ability to mother your child is called into question, it cuts like a knife!

After some time, and through much prayer and thought, my anger began to teach me some lessons. It wasn't important that I didn't have a chance to speak up for myself, and it wasn't important to prove myself to those strangers. What was important was the reminder it gave me. To be slow to speak and quick to show mercy. To allow my Father in heaven to do the judging and to try to understand that my neighbor might have been having a really bad day. To be understanding when I witness something that seems wrong, and to remind myself that I don't know everything. I actually tend to have empathy now, instead of criticism.

Yes, those who commit these random acts of judgment have become some of my greatest teachers. For that, I am forever grateful.

Megan Mileski

Together

Dear Mother,

To be honest, mother, I question almost everything I do with my kids. I wonder if I'm good enough, smart enough, wise enough, kind enough, hard enough. Do I spend enough time with them individually? Do I love them the way they need to be loved? Do I discipline them successfully? Am I pointing them to God in every moment? Am I growing men who will love and fear the Lord passionately? Men who will be honorable husbands? Men who will make the world a better place by their actions and words?

I wonder if you do the same, mother. Do we all second-guess ourselves? Maybe that's part of motherhood. My journey to being a mom took me on a crooked, winding path. It was not an easy one. I am a mother through adoption. I went through

Be thankful.
Be present.
Be amazed.

— Rebecca

a lot of pain on the way to my boys, and because of that, I look at motherhood through a different lens. Maybe you do too. We all have a story, don't we?

Because of the pain, the difficulty of adoption, I see things differently than I would have before. In the moments of utter frustration, I can look at my children and thank God for allowing me to be their mommy. I never thought I would be thankful for the grief I endured on my way to them, but at last I am. I don't know what kind of mother I would have been if I had delivered a baby nine months after we started trying to conceive. I'd like to think I'd be the same one I am now, but I have my doubts. When they were crying in the middle of the night, I was grateful for their presence—healthy, hungry boys who needed their mom. When they are fighting, I can (eventually) thank God for the fact that they have each other at all, not something I take for granted. I look into their eyes and stand in awe of the fact that they are my sons.

This is what I pray for you, mother. Whatever your path to motherhood was, I pray that you can take a moment to be in awe of your children and the fact that they *are* your children. That's not to say we can't or shouldn't get frustrated; children are ridiculously irritating at times. I think it's a gift to our children and ourselves, however, when we can look past the momentary struggles to the eternal value of what we're doing.

Let's do this together, mother, so we can know we're not alone when we feel overwhelmed or frustrated or defeated. You are not alone. Do you know that? Do you really know? *You are not alone.*

Be thankful. Be present. Be amazed.

You are loved.

In Him,

Rebecca Whitson

Crazy

Dear Mother,

Earlier this week I talked to a new friend. She's expecting her first baby in a few months, and she'd just had a terrible day full of hormones and emotions. She was wondering if she's crazy, because this being pregnant thing? It's not her favorite.

"No way," I reassured her. "You are not crazy."

She protested. Every mother she knows claims to have loved being pregnant, so surely there's something wrong with her. I promised her that no mother loves every second of her pregnancy, and some of us are miserable for a full nine months.

Isn't that just the way of motherhood, though? Thinking, *I must be crazy. Everyone else has it together. I'm the only one . . .*

I can't believe I fed my children cereal for breakfast, lunch, *and* dinner today.

Surely I'm the only mom who prays for her children to sleep past 7:00 a.m.

I bet nobody else loses their temper eight times before school starts.

It might be overkill, but I'm going to make sure she's still breathing. Again.

I just know the other moms have never screamed at their kids in the church parking lot.

The website said it could be chicken pox—or cancer. I'm just not sure.

I must be crazy.

You're not crazy. Well, you might be, but not for any of these things.

Something happens the moment you become a mother. The world becomes both more magical and more dangerous. Your body and your mind seem to be overtaken or, at the least, temporarily occupied by someone else—and you forget the last time you went an hour without being grabbed, pulled, pushed, or poked. And completing a conversation or train of thought becomes as elusive as a winning lottery ticket or long bath.

It's no wonder you feel a little crazy. But you're not. Not really. You've just joined the ranks of the sane but sleepy, rational but emotional, steady but sensitive women who call themselves mothers—no matter their different life situations or brand of crazy-but-not-crazy. These women know motherhood is hard and stressful and thankless and scary. It's almost enough to drive you crazy.

But it won't. You're not crazy. You're not alone. You're not the only one. You're not crazy.

Wishing you a full night's sleep and your own private bathroom break,

Mary Carver

Here

Dear Mother,

As Mommy to three young ones, I experience my fair share of long days, sleep-deprived nights, and extreme frustration. It seems obvious to me that crayon belongs on paper, not the walls, and that you can play with only so many toys at one time. But even in the craziest of moments, when there is laundry piled to the ceiling, dishes stacked on every counter, toys strewn about the entire house, and it's only nine in the morning, I try to remember that I could have missed all of this, and I choose to smile.

I could have missed every moment since my first baby was born. The resident who delivered me could not figure out why I did not stop bleeding. I have a picture of me holding my baby, but I don't remember it. I only remember my legs feeling so tired and heavy as I drifted off to sleep with my ashen husband at my side holding our minutes-old baby girl. I don't remember the more than twenty visitors who came into my room three hours later when the bleeding had become more managed, and I don't remember nursing my baby for the first time. I don't remember anything until she was fourteen hours old.

When she was seven weeks old, I nearly died of blood loss again. I faded away, pleading with the doctor to please not remove my female organs; I was only twenty-three and we wanted so many children. The last words I remember were the doctor's: "You will die if I don't stop this bleeding."

Transfusions and the removal of a large piece of retained placenta saved my life and my ability to bear children. And when our son was born via emergency C-section nearly three years later, I only cared that he was healthy despite being breech and three weeks early. But it happened again; the bleeding would not stop. Again a transfusion saved my life, and the doctor recommended we have no more children. We sadly agreed, but sometimes God has other plans.

By God's grace and the wisdom of my doctor, I safely carried and delivered our third blessing, without complication. And although we cannot have the five children we planned on, I am more than thankful for my three.

Tonight as I tucked my babies into bed, tripped over Hot Wheels, and folded laundry at midnight, I rejoiced over each peaceful face, each toy that we play with together, and each small piece of clothing that fits my small, little joys. A tear slipped down my cheek as I remembered that all too realistically, I could have missed this all.

And I don't want to miss a thing.

Love,

Carlee

The days are long but the years are not.

— Jessica

Notice

Dear Precious Mama,

Today I want you to know that you are not alone.

The dishes sitting on your counter—they are on mine too. The cereal mashed into your kitchen floor—those crumbs are on mine too. The laundry basket that is never empty—my basket is piled so full you can't see the basket.

This thing called motherhood is wondrous, but hard. And sometimes lonely. You wipe noses and tears, pick up superheroes and Barbie dolls, yet the littles always want more, don't they?

And it feels like no one notices. But I promise you, people do notice.

They notice when your child says thank you.

They notice when your child laughs with the joy that can only come from a happy home.

They notice when your child sweetly plays with a friend.

They notice that *you* are incredible.

You love well. You give generously. And most importantly, *you* shine the light of Jesus into the lives of those little souls God has given you.

Your legacy of mothering well will impact your child long after your time on this earth has ended. So take heart. Whisper prayers for strength and grace. And remember the old saying that the days are long but the years are not.

May you be blessed today, knowing that the Lord is your strength and that he believes in you—or else he wouldn't have made you a mother.

With love,

Jessica Turner

A Final Letter

The Truth in Weakness

Dear Mother,

I began this book with a letter about your powerful name. I call you "mother," because you are hard-core. Though you have bitten teeny tiny pieces of candy into quarters because you're terrified your child will choke to death, when it comes to other things, you are fearless. You could walk straight into any ghetto and hunt your baby down. You could dive into the depths of the ocean and punch a shark in the face. You could sit for hours next to a hospital bed like a huge anchor for a tiny boat being thrown about in a monsoon.

You are powerful, but there's a secret about where this power comes from. This kind of power only comes resurrection-style.

This is the kind of life that only happens on the other side of a dying—like how a plant doesn't grow unless the seed goes into the ground and dies there first.

When my boys were born, every single time, I was born new too. But first my body broke a little more, gone animal in childbirth. Even my mind left me. It was like I chipped up into great big puzzle pieces and came apart in the air, and when my mind came back to me, when the baby was drinking from my very body, the pieces of me came back together one by one in a new way, and there I was. A mother reborn.

Sometimes the dying is small. Four boys fighting or four boys playing, either way, I have to make a decision. Will my head blow right off the top of my body, or will I die to this and let peace remain even when I can't hear myself think?

Sometimes the dying is big. Sometimes it's a divorce or the loss of a child. Sometimes it's a terrible sickness or the loss of a dream. There's no way to know all the resurrections we'll experience when those babies come out naked and into our arms. We just know we're raw and broken in it all—so weak in our love.

Ours is a power that comes straight from weakness. Dear mother, you are weak.

You are weak, and your weakness is the very avenue for your greatness.

Don't forget to tell other mothers about it. Boast in your weakness. Resurrection power awaits.

You are not alone, fighting sharks and darkness, closet monsters and lies about scarcity! This is a great cloud of witnesses.

Listening with you,

Amber Haines

Contributing Mothers

Amber Oliver (Remember)
www.classichousewife.com
Twitter: @amberoliver

Amy Lyttle (Brokenness)

Ann Kroeker (Blink)
annkroeker.com
Twitter: @annkroeker

Becky Behling (Priestess)
movewitheasenow.com

Carrie Ferguson Weir (Fly)
bilingualintheboonies.com
tikitikiblog.com
Twitter: @carriefweir and
@tikitikiblog

Christy Brockman (Grace)

**Danielle Elliot Smith
(Surprises)**
extraordinarymommy.com
Twitter: @DanielleSmithTV

Elizabeth Walker (Real)

Grace Sandra (Courage)
gracesandra.com
Twitter: @Grace_Sandra_

Heather Manifold (Matched)
Twitter: @hmani

Jessica Turner (Notice)
www.themomcreative.com/
Twitter: @jessicanturner
Pinterest: JessicaNTurner

Joanne Newell (Kind)
www.richradiantreal.com
/blog
Twitter: @JoanneNewell

Kari Clark (Unexpected)

Kathy Werntz (Enjoy)

Katie Meyering (Victories)
alistmakerslife.com

Twitter: @listladykatie
Pinterest: listladykatie

Kristen Welch (Presence)
wearethatfamily.com
Twitter: @wearethatfamily
instagram:@wearethatfamily

Laura Bull (Worry)
garybull.blogspot.com

Leah England (Voice)

Lee Laughlin (Learn)
livefearlesslee.com
Twitter: @Fearless

Lisa Douglas (Cherish)
crazyadventuresinparenting
.com
Twitter: @crazyadventures

Lisa-Jo Baker (Anthem)
www.thegypsymama.com
Twitter: @thegypsymama

Lora Lynn Fanning (Being)
www.vitafamiliae.com
Twitter: @vitavamiliae

Mary Carver (Crazy)
www.givinguponperfect.com
Twitter: @marycarver

Megan Mileski (Empathy)
Twitter: @holditup

Meghan Matt (Blessed)
thefreebirdsings.com
Twitter: @meghanmatt

Mel Thompson (Learning)

Micha Boyett (Loved)
michaboyett.com
Twitter: @michaboyett

Mishelle Lane (Meltdown)
www.secretagentmama.com
www.mishellelanephoto
graphy.com

**Monica Daughters
(Mommy)**

Nish Weiseth (Seen)
nishweiseth.com
Twitter: @nishweiseth

**Patrice MacArthur
(Transformation)**
spiritualwomanthoughts
.blogspot.com

Rachel McAdams (Trust)

Rebecca Whitson (Together)
WhitsonLife.com
Twitter: @beccal1103

Robin Dance (Perfect)
pensieve.me
Twitter: @pensieverobin

Sarah Bessey (Calling)
sarahbessey.com
Twitter: @sarahbessey

Sarah Huaman (Growing)
iblamemom.blogspot.com
Twitter: @iblamemom

Sarah Hubmeier (Miracle)
oakbriarfarm.blogspot.com
Twitter: @SarahHub

Shannon Lowe (Shepherd)
rocksinmydryer.typepad
.com

Stephanie Bryant (Patience)

Stephanie Precourt (Super)
www.adventuresinbabywear
ing.com
Twitter: @babysteph

**Tammy Zufelt Thomas
(Queen)**

Tonia Peckover (Live)
studyinbrown.com

Wendy Joachim (Needing)

Amber C. Haines, author of *Wild in the Hollow*, is a soulful writer and blogger at TheRunaMuck.com and a regular contributor to DaySpring's (in)courage. She loves the church and finds community among the broken.

Seth Haines, author of *Coming Clean*, writes at SethHaines.com and is a regular contributor to various publications.

Seth and Amber make their home in the Arkansas Ozarks with their four boys.

Amber's soul-stirring memoir that traces her broken journey of finding the God who "haunts like wind in an Alabama hollow."

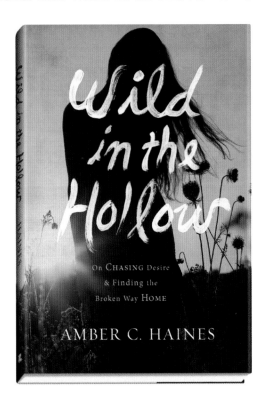

Connect with

AMBER

TheRunaMuck.com

Connect with

SETH

SethHaines.com